GOLF

GOLF

MASTERING THE BASICS WITH THE PERSONALIZED SPORTS INSTRUCTION SYSTEM

Michael Metzler
Georgia State University

Allyn and Bacon
Boston   London   Toronto   Sydney   Tokyo   Singapore

VICE PRESIDENT	Paul A. Smith
Publisher	Joseph E. Burns
EDITORIAL ASSISTANT	Annemarie Kennedy
MARKETING MANAGER	Rick Muhr
EDITORIAL PRODUCTION SERVICE	Bernadine Richey Publishing Services
TEXT DESIGN AND COMPOSITION	Barbara Bert Silbert
MANUFACTURING BUYER	Julie McNeill
COVER ADMINISTRATOR	Brian Gogolin

Copyright ©2001 by Allyn & Bacon
A Pearson Education Company
160 Gould Street
Needham Heights, MA 02494

All rights reserved. No part of the material protected by this copyright notice may be reproduced or utilized in any form or by any means, electronic or mechanical, including photocopying, recording, or by any information storage and retrieval system, without written permission from the copyright holder.

Internet: www.abacon.com

ISBN: 0-205-32386-3

Printed in the United States of America

10 9 8 7 6 5 4 3 2 1   05 04 03 02 01 00

CONTENTS

Preface	vii
MODULE 1 **STRETCHING FOR GOLF**	1
MODULE 2 **GOLF BASICS**	9
EQUIPMENT	10
GOLF COURSES	12
PAR	14
KEEPING SCORE IN GOLF	15
SWING BASICS	15
MODULE 3 **PUTTING**	29
STRAIGHT PUTTS	29
BREAKING PUTTS	39

MODULE 4 **COMPLETE GOLF SWING FOR BEGINNERS** 45

MODULE 5 **AROUND THE GREEN** 53
    CHIPPING 53
    PITCHING 61

MODULE 6 **APPROACH SHOTS WITH IRONS** 69

MODULE 7 **STARTING THE HOLE: TEE SHOTS** 83

MODULE 8 **SAND SHOTS FROM AROUND THE GREEN (OPTIONAL)** 95

MODULE 9 **GOLF KNOWLEDGE FOR BEGINNERS** 105
    GOLF RULES IN BRIEF 107
    WINTER RULES (UNOFFICIAL) 115
    PLAYING THROUGH 117
    GOLF KNOWLEDGE QUIZ 119

Personal Progress Chart for PSIS Golf 121

PREFACE

INTRODUCTION TO PSIS GOLF

Hello, and welcome to your **golf class**! That's right, *your* golf class. This personal workbook includes almost everything you will need to learn the game of golf and become a proficient beginning-level player. Of course, your instructor will play an important part as you progress, but most of what you will need is contained in your Personal Workbook. Your golf class will be taught this term using the **Personalized Sports Instruction System (PSIS)**, developed specifically for college basic instruction courses like the one in which you are enrolled. All of the materials in this workbook have been refined in field tests with many students like yourself, college men and women getting their first formal golf instruction.

The key design feature of the PSIS is that it permits for individualized learning and progression through the course. Think back to other classes you have taken: some students learn faster than others. This is a fact in all learning situations. Depending on individual learning rates, some students become frustrated if the course goes too fast. Others become bored if the course goes too slowly. Either way, many students become disinterested, reducing their enjoyment of the course. For golf, the most harmful result of frustration or boredom is that students are not given a proper chance to learn the game and to enjoy it as a regular part of their activity schedule. Whether you are a "bare beginner" or currently have some golf experience, the PSIS design will allow you to progress **"as quickly as you can, or as slowly as you need."** Keep this little motto in mind as you become familiar with this workbook and progress through your golf class this term.

Another point to keep in mind is that the PSIS is *achievement oriented*. That means the PSIS design is intended to help you learn the necessary skills, strategies, and rules for beginning golf play. I guarantee you will be a better player at the end of your PSIS class than you are now!

As you will see, your improvement will come in a way that is different from most other courses you have taken. You will be asked to assume more responsibility for your own learning than ever before. Remember, all the instructional material is included in your Personal Workbook. It will be up to you to learn the contents of the workbook, become familiar with the PSIS system, attend class regularly, follow your instructor's class policies, and work diligently toward completing the course sequences. It has been our experience that college students enjoy taking a large role in their own learning and appreciate the individualized plan of the PSIS. I know that you will, too.

ADVANTAGES OF THE PSIS FOR YOU

1. **The PSIS reduces your dependence on the instructor.** Your Personal Workbook provides nearly all the information you will need to complete the course. All content, learning task, and managerial information is at your fingertips, not with the instructor. When you are ready for a new learning task, the individualized plan will allow you to proceed on your own.

2. **Individualized learning is emphasized.** The PSIS will allow you to learn golf "as quickly as you can, or as slowly as you need." You will be able to remain in your own comfort zone while progressing through the course.

3. **You will have increased responsibility for your own learning.** As adult learners, college students can assume responsibility for much of their own learning. You can make decisions that have direct bearing on class atten-

dance, practice routines, and achievement. The PSIS system shifts much of the responsibility and decision making directly to you and away from the instructor.

4. **Your access to the instructor will be increased whenever you need it.** Since PSIS instructors can spend much more time in class teaching students, it means that you will get more personal attention and quality instruction, *that is, if you need it.* If you do not require as much interaction with the instructor, it will not be forced on you as with group learning strategies.

5. **You can chart your own progress.** Your PSIS Golf Personal Workbook includes a simple **Personal Progress Chart** to help you gauge your learning as you go through the course. This will help you to make decisions about your learning pace, projected grade, and how to use your class time most efficiently.

YOUR ROLE IN PSIS GOLF

Your role in PSIS Golf can be summarized easily: become familiar with and follow the Personal Workbook as an independent learning guide. You will not need to depend on the instructor for content and managerial information. But when the workbook is not sufficient or specific learning information is needed, you should be sure to *ASK FOR HELP!* Your Personal Workbook will provide nearly all the information needed to complete the course. So, if you can progress without the instructor's direction, the system is designed to let you. If you need help, the instructor will be free to provide it for you. Your instructor will show you a *help signal* for getting his or her attention in class. It might be a raised hand, a raised club, or a verbal call. Be sure you know this signal, and do not be shy about using it!

YOUR INSTRUCTOR'S ROLE IN PSIS GOLF

Your instructor has the important role of *facilitator* in your PSIS golf course. Your Personal Workbook will provide most of the content and management information you will need, providing your instructor more time to give students individual attention. There will be just one large-group demonstration throughout the entire course, and very little time will be spent organizing routine class "chores." Nearly all the instructor's time will be available to facilitate your learning on an individual basis.

Your instructor has the teaching experience and expertise to make the PSIS work as well as it was designed. The PSIS system allows the instructor to provide the maximum use of his or her expertise by *facilitating* the learning process for you.

SKILL AND KNOWLEDGE COURSE MODULES

Your PSIS golf course contains a number of learning activities divided into a series of modules. There are two types of modules: **performance skill** and **golf knowledge**. Performance skill modules focus on the major psychomotor performance patterns needed to play golf. The golf knowledge module contains information on basic game rules and golf etiquette.

PSIS COURSE MANAGEMENT AND POLICIES

In this section you will learn some of the ways in which the PSIS approach can give you increased control over your own learning. Some course management and policies will come from your Personal Workbook. Others will be communicated to you by your instructor. Be sure that you are familiar with all course management routines and policies.

1. **Dressing for class.** You will need to have proper clothing and footwear in order to participate comfortably and safely in your golf class. I suggest that you wear lightweight, loose-fitting clothes that will not restrict your range of motion (shorts, T-shirts, and the like). General-purpose court shoes or "cross training" shoes with soft soles are recommended. Specialized clothing and golf shoes are not necessary. Be sure to ask your instructor about his or her policies regarding dressing for class.

2. **Equipment.** Your instructor will provide you with all the necessary equipment for class, and with the routines for distributing and collecting equipment each day.

3. **Depositing and distributing Personal Workbooks.** Your instructor will advise you on his or her policy regarding your workbook each day after class. I suggest that the instructor collect all student workbooks at the end of class and bring them to class the next day. Be sure that you know the exact policy to be used, since you cannot participate fully in class without your own workbook.

4. **Practice partners.** Some learning tasks call for you to practice with one or more partners and be checked off by them. Any classmate can be your partner for most tasks. A few tasks will specify that all students in a drill be at the same place in the course learning sequence.

5. **Arriving to class** Your instructor will inform you about specific routines for arriving to class and beginning each day. Generally, you should (1) arrive at or before the class starting time, (2) locate your own Personal Workbook, (3) complete your stretching and warm-up routine, (4) find a practice partner (if needed at that time), and (5) begin to practice the appropriate learning task. Note that you can begin as soon as you arrive. Except for the first day of instruction, the instructor will not wait to begin the class with all students together. Arriving before class will allow you extra time to practice your golf skills.

6. **Self-checks, partner checks, and instructor checks.** Each learning task in PSIS golf requires that your mastery be documented (checked off). Some tasks can be checked off by you, some must be checked off by a partner, and some by your instructor. Items are checked off by the appropriate person initialing and dating the designated area after each checked task in your Personal Workbook. Instructor-checked tasks will require that you practice for a period of time prior to attempting mastery and being checked off. When you are ready, indicated by a series of successful trial blocks, signal the instructor again and ask him or her to observe you. If you do not reach the stated criterion, you can return for more practice and signal for the instructor at a later time. *There is no penalty for not making a mastery criterion. You can try as many times as it takes to be suc-*

cessful. You may find it helpful to alert the instructor at the beginning of a class in which you anticipate needing his or her observation and checking. The instructor will then be on the lookout for your signal.

7. **Grading.** Your course instructor will inform you about the grading system and related policies to be used in your PSIS golf class. Be sure you are aware of the specific requirements and procedures for determining your grade.

USING YOUR TIME EFFECTIVELY

Your PSIS golf course is made up of a series of predetermined learning tasks grouped into nine modules. Your course will have a set number of class days with a set class length. It is important for you to know your own learning pace and to make steady progress toward completing all course requirements. Therefore, you will need to learn how to best use your time in class and to accurately project completion of PSIS golf before the end of the term. Here are some helpful tips for managing your time.

1. Arrive to class early and begin right away. No signal will be given by the instructor for class to begin.

2. Stay for the entire class period. Do not get into a habit of leaving early.

3. Learn the PSIS course management system right away. The quicker you understand how it works, the sooner you can start using it to your advantage.

4. Do not hesitate to ask the instructor for assistance. Learn and use the class help signal to get the instructor's attention.

5. If there is not enough time to complete a new task in a class, at least *start* it. This will save time the next day.
6. When you are close to finishing a task at the end of a class, try to stay a few minutes late to complete it. This avoids repetitious setup time the next day and the possible loss of your learning momentum.

7. When a practice partner is needed, pair up with the first person you can find, rather than waiting for a certain person. (This is good way to get to know more of your classmates!)

8. Alert the instructor prior to instructor-checked criterion tasks so that he or she will be available when you need observation and a check-off.

PSIS GOLF LEARNING MODULES

This section will describe how the PSIS course learning modules are designed. It is important that you know how the PSIS works so that you can take advantage of its individualized learning features. The course learning content is included in two kinds of learning modules: **performance skill** and **golf knowledge**.

Each *performance skill* module will include the following:

1. A written **introduction** to the skill

2. An **instructor demonstration** of the proper skill techniques

3. Text and photographs that explain the **components** or **phases** of each skill

4. Photographs that highlight the key **performance cues** (these same cues will be presented by the instructor in his or her demonstration).

5. Simple **comprehension tasks** and **readiness drills** to develop initial skill patterns

6. An **error analysis** and **correction section** for self-analyzing common mistakes

7. **Learning tips** for increased proficiency

8. A series of several **criterion tasks** for practicing and demonstrating your skill mastery

9. One or more **challenge tasks** for developing tactical applications of skills in modified competitive situations

10. A **Personal Recording Form** for selected tasks, used to record successful practice trials

The *golf knowledge* module includes the following:

1. A **reading** on the basic rules of golf and golf game strategy

2. A **knowledge quiz** to test your understanding of the rules and strategy

CHARTING YOUR PROGRESS

The last page of your PSIS golf workbook includes your **Personal Progress Chart**. Your instructor will show you how to correctly label the chart, and the rest is very simple. At the end of each week in the course, put an x above that date, and across from the last task you completed. As the weeks go by, you will begin to see how your individual learning pace projects your successful completion of all course learning modules.

This introductory section, combined with additional information from your instructor, will allow you to use the PSIS golf workbook to your full advantage and to learn golf at your own pace, with highly individualized attention from your instructor. Because PSIS golf is a complete system for learning the game, it might take you a little time to become familiar with this approach. However, remember that your instructor is there to help when you have questions about the system and when you need individual attention for learning. Now that you know about the PSIS golf system, you are probably anxious to get started. I hope you enjoy learning golf with the PSIS approach and that you will become an avid player of this lifelong game. READY...SET...GO!!

MODULE 1

STRETCHING FOR GOLF

INTRODUCTION

Flexibility refers to the ability of the muscles, tendons, and ligaments around a joint to move, while providing support and allowing the joint to move smoothly through its entire range of motion. Increased flexibility means more supple muscles, which reduces the risk of injury to the muscle when the limb is moved suddenly. The static method is the most commonly recommended stretching technique. It has been shown to be extremely effective in increasing range of motion and, when done slowly and carefully, presents little chance of injury to the muscles.

Some sports and forms of exercise lead to improved flexibility of the involved body part. Golf, for example, tends to limber the shoulder joint and lower back. Gymnastics can only be accomplished with a high degree of flexibility in virtually all points of the body. Activities such as walking and jogging do not require a large range of motion and do not increase flexibility. This is why it is important that stretching should precede these types of exercises. Stretching not only enhances performance, but also reduces the risk of injury.

Flexibility should be included during the warm-up phase of an exercise program. This allows for gentle stretching of muscles around the joint before vigorous movement and leads to a slower cool-down, thereby maintaining local blood flow and reducing postexercise soreness.

Although muscular soreness can have many origins, one major cause appears to be damage to the connective tissue elements in the muscles and tendons. No one method of overcoming soreness is available, but adequate stretching appears to aid not only in preventing soreness, but also in relieving it when it already exists.

PERFORMANCE CUES

1. **Warm-up.** Protect the muscle by beginning with a low- to moderate-intensity warm-up for 2 to 3 minutes prior to performing strenuous stretching exercises. Running in place or a brisk walk should provide an excellent warm-up.
2. **Do not bounce.** Move into the stretching position slowly, continuing until mild tension is felt. Utilize a static or very slow stretch and hold the position. A ballistic or bouncing stretch can be counterproductive and even cause injury.
3. **Hold the stretch.** The stretch position should be held for a predetermined amount of time. It is suggested that the initial holding position be between 15 and 20 seconds and gradually increased over the following weeks. As flexibility improves, attempt to hold the stretch slightly longer. When the stretching exercise is complete, the body the body should be released slowly from the stretch position.
4. **Target zone.** You should not feel pain when stretching a muscle. In the stretching target zone, *there is tension in the muscle without pain.* It is important to be aware of your own target zone. Stretching at a level below the target zone will not lead to increased flexibility, whereas stretching above this zone will increase the risk of injury.
5. **Breathing.** Do not hold your breath while stretching. Breathing should be slow, rhythmical, and continuous.
6. **Stretch before and after exercise.** Stretching before vigorous exercise prepares the muscles and joint for activity and reduces the risk of injury. Stretching after vigorous exercise is needed to further stretch the muscles. Both warm-up and cool-down are needed.

STRETCHING FOR GOLF

INSTRUCTOR DEMONSTRATION

Your course instructor will demonstrate each recommended stretching exercise for golf. Observe the demonstration carefully, making note of the performance cues for each exercise.

Shoulder Stretch (triceps). Elevate one elbow and position the club down the middle of your back. Reach behind your back with the other hand and grab the club slightly above belt-high. Gently apply force by moving the bottom hand down, causing your other elbow to rise (and stretch). Hold the stretch in the target zone for 15 to 20 seconds and slowly release. Refer to Photos 1.1A and B. Repeat this exercise 5 to 8 times with both shoulders.

Photo 1.1A
Shoulder stretch, back view

Photo 1.1B
Shoulder stretch, side view

Lateral Shoulder Stretch. Elevate the arms and grip the club near each end. Gently pull down with one arm, stretching the opposite shoulder. Bend your hips in the direction of the pull. Knees should be slightly flexed during the exercise. Hold the stretch in the target zone for 15 to 20 seconds and slowly release. Refer to Photos 1.2A and B. Repeat this exercise 5 to 8 times on both sides of the body.

Photo 1.2A
Lateral stretch to left

Photo 1.2B
Lateral stretch to right

Lower Back and Hamstrings Stretch. From a standing position and holding the club near each end, bend forward at the hips and allow the head and arms to hang downward. Have both knees slightly flexed during this exercise. Hold the stretch in the target zone for 15 to 20 seconds and slowly release. Refer to Photos 1.3A and B. Repeat this exercise 5 to 8 times.

Photo 1.3A
Lower back and hamstrings stretch, front view

Photo 1.3B
Lower back and hamstrings stretch, side view

MODULE 1

Weighted Warm-up Swings. You can use a weight designed to fit on the end of a golf club, or use three or four clubs gripped as a bunch. Assume a balanced stance and SLOWLY swing the club(s) back and forth in a pendulum, increasing the arc of the pendulum every four swings, until you get to a full backswing and follow-through. Refer to Photos 1.4A through C. Be sure to do this stretch slowly, gently, and with an even arc; be cautious not to swing too hard.

Photo 1.4A
Starting point

STRETCHING FOR GOLF   7

Photo 1.4B
Backswing

Photo 1.4C
Frontswing

CRITERION TASK 2-1

Partner-Checked

Pair up with another person in the class. In turn, perform each stretch while the other observes for proper technique. Have your partner check and initial below when you have performed each stretch just as your instructor demonstrated. If you have questions or need assistance, use the help signal to alert your instructor.

1. Shoulder stretch
2. Lateral shoulder stretch
3. Lower back and hamstrings stretch
4. Weighted warm-up swings

Partner's initials _____ Date completed _____

MODULE 2

GOLF BASICS

INTRODUCTION

Golf is one of the world's oldest games, originating in Scotland over 300 years ago. It was intended as a sporting game based on skill, strategy, some risk taking, and a constant challenge between a player, an opponent, the elements of nature, and the golf course itself. Many avid golfers will admit that their own attraction for the game comes from the ever-changing challenges faced each time the game is played, even in familiar settings.

The playing of golf has changed dramatically in just the past 10 years. It is now being taken up by many groups of people who were previously not attracted to it or did not have the opportunity to play: I refer to girls, women, young men, and minorities. The game of golf is experiencing unprecedented growth in the United States and around the world today. Some of that is attributable to the "Tiger Woods phenomenon," but most of it is due to the increased access to golf for the middle-income earners and inner-city populations. Golf is not just a game for affluent white men anymore. Perhaps this is what attracted you to enroll in a formal golf class at your university.

Regardless of your motivation to learn golf, you likely share one characteristic with the thousands of new players who take up golf each year: you want to develop your skills and knowledge of the game to a point that will allow you to enjoy golf to its fullest and to play at a level that suits you. To get to this point, you will need to start with the basics, and this is where your PSIS golf class begins.

EQUIPMENT

There are several basic equipment needs for beginning golf play. More advanced players will have a longer list of equipment needs and require more specialized equipment. The complicated part of learning about golf equipment is that there is a mind-boggling array of choices for every type of equipment, with a wide range of prices. I recommend that you do not purchase any equipment for your introductory course. Your instructor will be able to tell you about the kind of equipment you will need and offer some suggestions for how to select each type. You will have a much better idea of what your equipment needs are once you have finished this course and have learned your own unique swing pattern.

GOLF CLUBS

Golf club design and the materials from which clubs are made have become high tech today. Each manufacturer claims to have clubs with unique designs and built from the latest materials. These claims may or may not be true. However, you will be relieved to know that all golf clubs share many similar design and materials characteristics, so as a beginning player you need to know only a few basics about clubs.

A set of golf clubs consists of four types: irons, woods, wedges, and a putter. Irons and woods are identified by a numbering system that indicates a different length and loft for each club. The club with the lowest number is the longest and has the least loft, indicating that it will produce a lower, longer shot. As the club numbers increase, each club will be a bit shorter and have a bit more loft, so clubs with a higher number produce shorter and higher shots. Woods are typically numbered 1 (or *driver*) to 5. Irons are typically numbered 3 to 9. Now, the tricky part is that in modern golf a wood is not made of wood at all! Clubs that were previously made of wood are now made with high-tech metal alloys, but the name *wood* has remained in the terminology of golf. Wedges are very short clubs used to produce shots that travel short distances with maximum loft, allowing the ball to land softly on the landing area near the hole. Wedges come in a few varieties: a pitching wedge, a lofted or L-wedge, and a sand wedge. Each type has a unique application, which will be discussed in later modules.

The putter is the shortest club. It has a flat face that produces zero lift on the ball so that the ball rolls on the putting surface at all times. Putters come in a wide variety of designs and materials. Selection is made based on the personal preference of each player.

GOLF BALLS

Manufacturers of golf balls also make many claims about the design and materials used to make their balls. Golf balls are made with a variety of characteristics that can produce more control, longer distance, and more loft. But, for the beginning player, none of these should be of concern. At this point you only need to know that most golf balls are white in color and can be used many times.

GOLF GLOVES

A thin leather glove is worn on the nondominant hand by many players today. The glove is used to increase friction while gripping the club and to protect against blisters. Gloves come in a variety of colors and sizes to fit snugly on any player's hand.

GOLF SHOES

Specialized shoes are worn by most players today. Golf shoes are designed to improve stability during a swing and to prevent sliding, which can cause a loss of control and even injury. Traditional golf shoes have a set of small metal spikes on the soles. The latest style of shoes has shorter, rubberlike cleats, called *soft spikes*. The soft-spiked shoe is now preferred by most golf facilities because they do not make marks on the putting surface, as does the traditional spike.

TEES

A simple but very useful piece of equipment is the tee. A tee is a short wooden peg placed in the ground, on which the ball is placed for the first shot of each hole. A teed ball is easier to hit than a ball resting on the ground, so players will use a tee whenever the rules allow.

GOLF COURSES

The game of golf is played on a golf course. A golf course is a tract of land designed specifically for this game. A course includes natural features such as grass, sand, water, trees, and other foliage. Some of these features are used to make a course visually appealing, whereas others are used to make a course more challenging. Modern golf course design is creative and sometimes unusual, but all golf courses share several common characteristics in the layout. All regulation courses have 18 holes. Each hole includes a designated starting spot (the *tee box*), one or more obstacles, defined boundaries, a certain distance to the putting surface (the green), and the cup (target) with a flagstick in it. The flagstick is used to sight the cup as the player hits toward the green.

TEE BOX AND TEE MARKERS

Each hole has a starting place, the tee box. It is a flat, level area. The tee box has two markers on it that designate the specific place from which players begin the hole. Play on the hole must start between the tee markers and no more than two club lengths back from them. Players are allowed to use a tee when making their first shot on each hole. This is the only time a ball may be teed on the hole.

FAIRWAY

The preferred landing area between the tee box and putting green is the fairway. The fairway area is typically the shortest path to the green from the tee box, and the grass is trimmed to an optimal height for making accurate shots.

ROUGH

The rough is a stretch of longer grass on one or both sides of the fairway. Because the grass is longer, it is more difficult to make shots from the rough than from the fairway. There is no penalty for landing in the rough, but it is not the preferred place to be when trying to hit to the putting green.

SAND TRAPS

Sand traps, or bunkers, are areas adjacent to the fairway or the putting green filled with sand. The element of sand greatly increases the difficulty of making shots. There is no penalty for landing in a sand trap, but doing so almost always results in one or more extra strokes on the hole.

OUT-OF-BOUNDS AREA

Many golf holes have an out-of-bounds area, designated by white stakes visible to the player. If the ball lands outside the white stakes, the player must count that shot, add a one stroke penalty, and rehit the next shot from the original spot. This is referred to as a *stroke-and-distance penalty.*

LATERAL HAZARDS

Lateral hazards are designated by red stakes on the golf hole. The hazard could be a body of water, a stream, or a wooded area. If a ball lands in a lateral hazard, a player has two options. If the ball can be stroked, the player can take the next shot from this spot with no penalty. If the ball cannot be stroked from the hazard, the player must add a one-stroke penalty and take the next shot from behind the point where the ball entered the hazard, but no closer to the hole. This is referred to as a *stroke penalty*.

PUTTING GREEN

Each hole has a putting green at the end of it. The green can be large or small and of almost any shape. It will likely have many undulations. The grass on the green is trimmed closely to the ground, allowing the ball to roll smoothly.

CUP AND FLAG STICK

The target on each hole is the cup. A hole is complete when a player rolls her or his ball into the cup. The cup can be located anyplace on the green. The cup has a flag stick in it to help players sight the cup as they approach the green. The flag stick must be removed when playing shots from the green. The flag is also used by players to help determine the strength and direction of any wind when making shots to the green.

PAR

Each hole has a par rating, indicating the standard number of shots it should take to complete the hole. Adding up par for all 18 holes determines the par score for each golf course, commonly set at 72. In general, a hole's par rating is based on the distance from tee to green. Short holes have a par rating of 3, medium-distance holes a par rating of 4, and the longest holes a par rating of 5. A player's score on a hole can be referred to by the number of strokes it takes to finish or by this number's relationship to par.

2 under par	=	eagle
1 under par	=	birdie
at par	=	par
1 over par	=	bogie
2 over par	=	double bogie, and so on

KEEPING SCORE IN GOLF

Golf can be played in a variety of formats and scoring systems. The most common format is stroke play, in which each attempted shot counts in a player's score. The object, then, is to complete the 18 holes by taking the fewest strokes and having the lowest score. The Golf Knowledge Module will familiarize you with the rules of stroke play, but for now you should understand that the primary objective in golf is to take the fewest strokes possible on each of the 18 holes. Adding penalty strokes for landing in hazards and out-of-bounds areas raises a player's score, thus placing a premium on the ability to hit golf shots accurately. This ability is developed by knowing and executing the fundamentals of the golf swing, as covered in the next section.

SWING BASICS

As you just learned, the primary objective in golf is to complete a round of 18 holes with the fewest strokes. How you swing on each stroke leads directly to the outcome of each shot. To score well in golf, it is essential to develop a consistently good swing pattern, producing accurate shots that allow you to play from the fairway as often as possible. A good golf shot begins with the proper *setup*. **How you setup on each shot is the most important factor in getting good results.** The setup is comprised of eight interrelated components: (1) grip, (2) stance, (3) ball placement, (4) hand (grip) alignment, (5) clubface alignment, (6) aiming line, (7) swing path, and (8) club selection. The following sections provide you with drawings and photographs to explain the purpose and function of each component. Your instructor will refer to and demonstrate each component (called a *performance cue*) as it is needed for each golf shot you learn.

The key for a proper setup is to know how to execute each component and how it will affect your results. Many common errors for beginners are not swing errors. Rather, they are errors that result from improper setup **before** the shot is attempted.

GRIP

How your hands grip the club is the first key component for the setup. The two main purposes of the grip are: (1) to provide a comfortable hold on the club and (2) to allow both hands to work as a single unit when executing the swing. Two common grips are used in golf: the *overlapping* grip and the *interlocking* grip. Your instructor will demonstrate both grips to you, and you can refer to Photos 2.1A and B and 2.2A and B for pictures of each. Note that both grips look similar from the top view, so you will need to take careful note of the bottom views. Either grip can be used for shots off the green, but the overlapping grip is commonly used for putting. Most players today use the interlocking grip off the green.

Photo 2.1A
Overlapping grip, bottom view (turned up)

Photo 2.1B
Overlapping grip, top view

GOLF BASICS 17

Photo 2.2A
Interlocking grip, bottom view (turned up)

Photo 2.2B
Interlocking grip, top view

MODULE 2

STANCE

The stance refers to how your feet are aligned in the setup. In all cases your feet should be **at shoulder-width or slightly farther apart**. Your instructor will demonstrate the proper knee, back, and head alignment for each type of shot. You can use three basic stance alignments for your feet: (1) *square*, (2) *open*, and (3) *closed*. Most shots call for a square stance, so be sure you know how to set up with that one. Refer to Photos 2.3 through 2.5 for a picture of each stance. In each photo, the club shaft represents the *aiming line*, a straight line to your target.

Photo 2.3
Square stance

GOLF BASICS 19

Photo 2.4
Open stance

Photo 2.5
Closed stance

MODULE 2

BALL PLACEMENT

Ball placement is a combination of two things: (1) how far you set your feet away from the ball and (2) the relationship of the ball to your body's midline. The midline is an imaginary line that divides you into left and right halves. It extends vertically through your body at your naval. When using irons, the ball is placed slightly forward of your midline (Photo 2.6). When using woods, the ball is placed just behind the heel of your front foot (Photo 2.7).

Photo 2.6
Ball placement for irons

GOLF BASICS **21**

Photo 2.7
Ball placement for woods

HAND ALIGNMENT

Hand alignment is similar to ball placement. It refers to the relationship of your gripped hands to the midline of your body and the ball. Hand alignment affects a shot's loft: the farther "out front" you place your hands, the lower the ball will fly. Photos 2.8 and 2.9 demonstrate the two most common hand alignments: *midline* and *forward*.

CLUBFACE ALIGNMENT

Each club has a hitting surface on it, the *clubface*. The alignment of the clubface at setup largely determines the alignment of the clubface when the ball is contacted, giving each shot its direction and loft. The three common club-

Photo 2.8
Hands on mid-line

Photo 2.9
Hands forward

face alignments are *square* (perpendicular to the aiming line), *open* (turned out from the aiming line), and *closed* (turned in from the aiming line). Nearly all golf shots require a square clubface, so it is important to be able to use this alignment well.

A *square alignment* (Photo 2.10) results in a shot that follows the aiming line directly to the target, and **with the amount of loft designed for the selected club**. An *open alignment* (Photo 2.11) causes the ball to start inside the aiming line and *fade* to the target **with increased loft and reduced roll**. A *closed alignment* (Photo 2.12) will cause the ball to start out across the aiming line and *draw* back to the target **with reduced loft and increased roll**. Fade and draw shots are beyond the skill ability of most beginning golfers, so it is strongly recommended that you use a square clubface alignment for this course, and experiment with the other alignments when you have more proficiency and control.

24 MODULE 2

Photo 2.10
Square clubface

Photo 2.11
Open clubface

GOLF BASICS **25**

Photo 2.12
Closed clubface

AIMING LINE

The aiming line is an imaginary line drawn from the ball to the target. It indicates the exact direction you want your ball to travel. For tee shots, your aiming line is to the middle of the fairway. For approach shots to the green your aiming line is to the flag stick. For short and straight putts, your aiming line is directly to the middle of the cup. For breaking (curving) putts, chip shots, and pitch shots your aiming line depends on the amount of curve you anticipate the ball will have when it begins rolling on the green. Adjustments to the aiming line and how to determine *break* will be covered in later modules. For now, consider your aiming line to be straight at your target (see Illustration 2.1).

MODULE 2

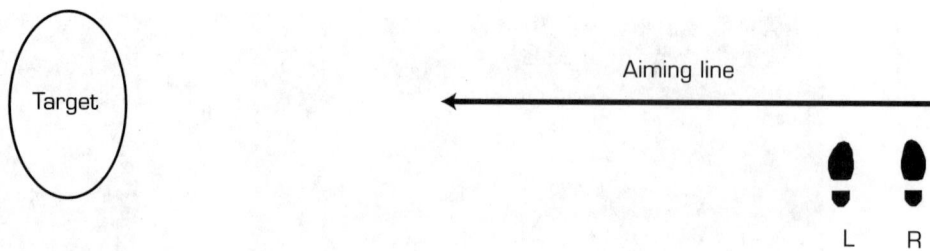

Illustration 2.1
Aiming line to target

SWINGPATH

The swing path is an imaginary line along which the clubhead travels in the backswing, front swing, and after contact with the ball. Although it is not physically possible to keep the clubhead on the aiming line for the entire backswing and follow-through, it is very important to keep it on the aiming line at the bottom of the swing, as the club moves forward and makes contact. Refer to Illustration 2.2. It is easiest to understand the swing path in

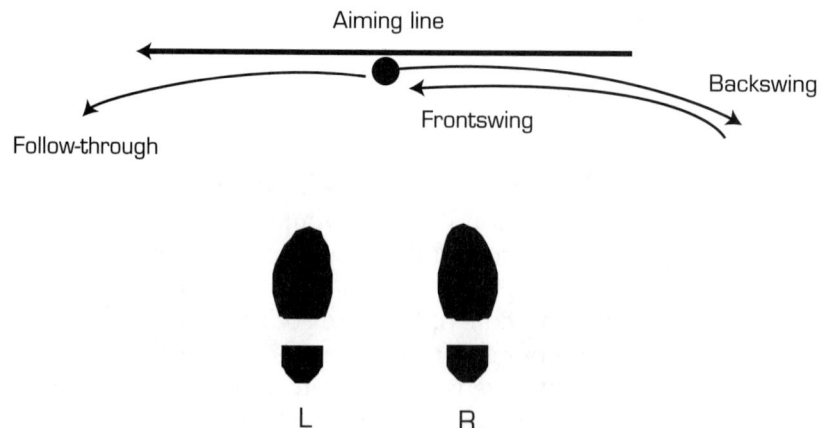

Illustration 2.2
Swing path

relationship to the **aiming line**. For nearly all shots, it is best to keep your swing path on the aiming line as much as possible, especially at the bottom of your swing.

CLUB SELECTION

Because a set of golf clubs includes clubs with different lofts and lengths, one of the most important decisions a player makes on every shot is selecting the best club for the needs of that shot. Selection depends on the distance you need to hit the ball and the amount of loft you wish the ball to travel with. Remember, higher loft results in less roll once the ball lands, giving you more control over your results.

The PSIS approach "teaches by distance, not by clubs." This means that you will learn what club you need for each distance, rather than trying to hit the same distance as your classmates with a certain club. To hit a shot 150 yards, some students can use a 7-iron, while other students will need a much longer club with less loft, a 4-iron perhaps. It is very important that you understand three things when selecting a club for each shot: (1) the designed purpose for each club; (2) the differences between clubs for length and loft, and (3) how far and high **you** can hit with each club.

COMPREHENSION TASK

Find a partner for this task. Get a middle-iron (5-, 6-, or 7-iron) and one golf ball. Find an open space in the practice area, safely away from other groups. Once there, determine a target to aim at (although you will not hit a ball to it). In turn, each partner will demonstrates the following techniques while the other partner observes for correct execution. The observing partner calls out the name of the technique, and the other partner demonstrates it. Have your partner check off each correct technique you perform and then initial and date to verify your completion of this task. This task is complete when both partners correctly execute all the techniques on the list.

MODULE 2

1. Overlapping grip _____
2. Interlocking grip _____
3. Square stance _____
4. Open stance _____
5. Closed stance _____
6. Ball placement, irons _____
7. Ball placement, woods _____
8. Midline hands _____
9. Forward hands _____
10. Square clubface _____
11. Open clubface _____
12. Closed clubface _____
13. Swingpath _____

   (Slow motion, no ball)

Partner's initials _____   Date _____

MODULE 3

PUTTING

The putting technique is used when your ball rests on (or very near) the green and you are trying to roll the ball into the cup. While the putt is the "smallest swing," it is the most important shot for good scoring. Remember that each short putt counts as much on your score as any other (and much longer) shot. An old golf saying goes, "You drive for show and putt for dough," meaning that the ability to putt well is better for lowering your score than the ability to hit the ball long. The putt is also the basic building block for all other swing techniques, so by mastering this stroke you are on your way to learning the foundation for every other type of swing.

STRAIGHT PUTTS

As you will learn, few golf putts will allow you to take an aiming line straight at the cup. Most putts curve, or break, as they roll to the cup. However, the ability to hit longer, breaking putts is built on the skill to hit putts that are short and straight, so this is where you will start.

MODULE 3

INSTRUCTOR DEMONSTRATION

Your course instructor will provide you with an explanation and demonstration of the key performance cues for the putting stroke. If you have questions, be sure to ask them before proceeding to the individualized task sequence. Refer to Photos 3.1A through E as your instructor explains and demonstrates each performance cue for the putting stroke.

Photo 3.1A
Putt stance, side view

PUTTING **31**

Photo 3.1B
Putt stance, front view

Photo 3.1C
Backswing

32 MODULE 3

Photo 3.1D
Contact point

Photo 3.1E
Follow-through

SETUP AND PERFORMANCE CUES

1. **Club:** Putter
2. **Grip:** Overlapping preferred, but interlocking acceptable
3. **Stance:** Square, with slight bend at knees (locked), bend at back, "nose over ball"
4. **Ball placement:** On midline, or slightly forward (one ball width)
5. **Hands alignment:** On midline
6. **Clubface:** Square to the hole (perpendicular to aiming line)
7. **Aiming line:** Straight to the middle of the hole
8. **Swing path:** Straight back and forth on aiming line
9. **Follow-through:** Make your follow through the same length as your backswing; keep the putter head on the aiming line during the entire swing

COMPREHENSION TASK

Find a partner and demonstrate to each other the proper performance cues for the putting stroke *without hitting the ball*. Be sure to provide feedback to each other for correct and incorrect performance cues until both of you can correctly execute this stroke.

LEARNING TIPS

1. Use a grip with firm (locked) wrists, but don't squeeze the club too hard.
2. Use a pendulum swing motion with equal length and even tempo for backswing and follow-through.
3. Your follow through should go past your front foot, directly on the aiming line.
4. Use a *swing triangle* (both shoulders and gripped hands) to swing; do not flex your wrists or bend your elbows on the swing.
5. Keep the clubhead on the aiming line for the entire backswing and follow-through.

READINESS DRILLS

3-1. Get 6 to 8 golf balls and find a place on the putting practice area. Using the proper putting stance and techniques, hit 50 putts, trying to make good contact with the ball. **Do not aim for a hole.** You should be trying to develop a feel for how far the ball will travel as it rolls on the green. Do not be concerned with accuracy at this time.

3-2. Find a place on the putting practice area and pick two spots on the green, both on the same aiming line. Make sure that the aiming line is not on a slope that will cause the ball to curve as it rolls. One spot should be about 10 feet away and the other spot should be about 20 feet away. Hit alternating putts to each spot, trying to keep the ball on the aiming line as closely as possible. Hit 20 putts to each spot.

If you experience difficulty with these readiness drills, refer to the **Performance Cues** and review each cue as presented. If you still have difficulty, ask your course instructor to assist you in applying these techniques.

Common Errors and Their Correction

Error	**Correction**
Punching the ball (hitting it hard with no follow-through). This results in erratic distance: very short one time, very long the next.	1. Make backswing and follow-through the same length and (even) speed. 2. Have putter follow through past front foot.
Peeking (lifting your head before follow-through is complete). This results in inconsistent errors; sometimes way right, sometimes way left, sometimes *topping* the ball.	Complete follow-through, count 1... 2, then lift head.
Pushing. The clubhead is inside the aiming line on backswing, then outside the aiming line on follow-through. This results in the ball missing away from your side of the hole.	1. Usually caused by incorrect backswing. 2. Start (and keep) clubhead over correct aiming line, especially on the backswing.

Common Errors and Their Correction (continued)

Error	Correction
Pulling. The clubhead is outside the aiming line on backswing, then inside the aiming line on follow-through. This results in the ball missing to your side of the hole.	1. Usually caused by incorrect backswing. 2. Start (and keep) clubhead over correct aiming line, especially on the backswing.

CRITERION TASKS FOR STRAIGHT PUTTS

Find a place on the putting practice area with an open cup to aim for. More than one student can be aiming at the same cup, so you will likely have to share a cup. Find a cup that is on a level, flat area so that the ball will not curve when it rolls. Do not attempt to make the mastery criterion right away for each new task. Hit putts until you become consistent, and then try to reach the mastery criterion.

CRITERION TASK 3-1

Self-Checked

1. *Distance from hole:* Two feet
2. *Target:* Holed putt
3. *Criterion:* Make 10 consecutive putts, 2 times

Practice this task in blocks of 10 putts. Record the number of successful putts in each block on the **Personal Recording Form.** When two block scores reach 10 (does not have to be consecutive blocks), initial and date in the space provided.

Personal Recording Form

Block 1	Block 2	Block 3	Block 4	Block 5	Block 6	Block 7	Block 8	Block 9	Block 10
___/10	___/10	___/10	___/10	___/10	___/10	___/10	___/10	___/10	___/10

Your initials _____   Date completed _____

CRITERION TASK 3-2

Self-Checked

1. *Distance from hole:* 4 feet
2. *Target:* Holed putt
3. *Criterion:* Make 7 of 10 putts, 3 times

Practice this task in blocks of 10 putts. Record the number of successful putts in each block on the **Personal Recording Form**. When three block scores reach or exceed 7 (does not have to be consecutive blocks), initial and date in the space provided.

Personal Recording Form

Block 1	Block 2	Block 3	Block 4	Block 5	Block 6	Block 7	Block 8	Block 9	Block 10
___/10	___/10	___/10	___/10	___/10	___/10	___/10	___/10	___/10	___/10

Your initials _____   Date completed _____

CRITERION TASK 3-3

Self-Checked

1. *Distance from hole:* 8 feet
2. *Target:* Holed putt, or stop within 1 foot of hole (any direction)
3. *Criterion:* Inside target 7 of 10 putts, 3 times

Practice this task in blocks of 10 putts. Record the number of successful putts in each block on the **Personal Recording Form**. When three block scores reach or exceed 7 (does not have to be consecutive blocks), initial and date in the space provided.

Personal Recording Form									
Block 1	Block 2	Block 3	Block 4	Block 5	Block 6	Block 7	Block 8	Block 9	Block 10
__/10	__/10	__/10	__/10	__/10	__/10	__/10	__/10	__/10	__/10

Your initials _____   Date completed _____

CRITERION TASK 3-4

Instructor-Checked

1. *Distance from hole:* 12 feet
2. *Target:* Holed putt, or stop within 2 feet of hole (any direction)
3. *Criterion:* Inside target 7 of 10 putts, 3 times

Practice this task in blocks of 10 putts. Record the number of successful putts for each block on the **Personal Recording Form**. When your block scores regularly approach or exceed 7 out of 10, ask your instructor to observe and witness your reaching of criterion. When your instructor has observed three successful blocks, he or she will initial and date in the space provided.

Personal Recording Form									
Block 1	Block 2	Block 3	Block 4	Block 5	Block 6	Block 7	Block 8	Block 9	Block 10
___/10	___/10	___/10	___/10	___/10	___/10	___/10	___/10	___/10	___/10

Instructor's initials _____ Date completed _____

BREAKING PUTTS

INTRODUCTION

Most putting greens are not flat, level surfaces. They have slope and undulations that are there by design. This feature adds an extra dimension to the skill of putting; not only do you need to hit the ball with the proper speed, but you must also determine the exact *aiming line* to take as the ball rolls toward the cup. This line is rarely directly at the cup itself. It is usually to an imaginary spot to the right or left of the cup. Any putt that will curve on its way to the cup is said to *break*. The larger the curve, the more break the putt has.

READING THE BREAK

There are two key things to recognize on every putt: *distance* (so that you know how hard you must hit the putt to reach the hole, but not go too far past if it misses), and *break* (how much curve and the direction of the curve the ball will take as it rolls toward the cup). You already have developed some feel for judging distance and the proper speed needed for putts of different lengths. *Reading* a break means determining both the direction (right or left) and the amount of break (the distance the ball will curve on the way to the cup). You must *read the putt* before you take your stance and establish your aiming line to the *target* which will be an imaginary spot to the right of left of the cup, and not the cup itself. This is what makes hitting breaking putts difficult for novice players: you will take an aiming line that is not directly to the cup, but you cannot know exactly how far to the right or left it will be! And there is one more complicating factor you will soon learn: the speed of the rolling ball affects how much of the break comes into play. Slow-rolling putts curve more than faster-rolling putts. So the problem becomes two-dimensional: trying to determine how fast to hit the putt and and how much it will break at that speed, knowing that incorrect speed will cause it to break less or more than you anticipated. (It is no wonder that professional golfers spend more than half of their entire practice time on putting!)

PERFORMANCE CUES

1. Crouch down about 6 feet behind your ball, facing the cup.
2. Identify the slope between your ball and the cup. (Which side of the green is higher, right or left?)
3. If the left side is higher, the putt will *break to the right*. Aim to the left of the hole.
4. If the right side is higher, the putt will *break to the left*. Aim to the right of the hole.
5. Determine the severity of the slope in the green. The more severe the slope, the more the ball will break on its way to the hole.
6. Determine how hard you need to hit the ball to get it to the cup, but not roll more than 2 feet past if the putt misses.
7. If the putt needs to be hit hard, anticipate less break. If the putt needs to be hit softly, anticipate more break.
8. Determine your aiming line and identify a spot on the green about halfway to the cup and on that line. Keep this spot in your vision as you assume your stance and take an aiming line to the spot.
9. Hit your putt at your calculated speed on your aiming line and over your target spot. DO NOT AIM TO THE CUP.
10. Take a good stance and hit your putt as if it was a straight putt *to the target spot*.

COMPREHENSION TASK

With a partner, drop several balls onto the green, at various distances around a cup. For each ball, determine the direction and (relative) amount of break and compare your observations. Always state the relative amount of the break (a little, a lot) and the direction (left or right). Do this until both partners agree on five "reads" in a row.

LEARNING TIPS

1. The amount of break will change with the speed with which you hit the putt. The **slower** the ball travels, the more it will break. The **faster** it travels, the less it will break.

2. Change nothing from what you learned about straight putts except the aiming line.

READINESS DRILLS

3-3. From various distances, attempt 25 putts that break to the right and 25 that break to the left, using different speeds from each distance. Do not be concerned with accuracy; use these putts to learn the relationship between slope, distance, and speed on breaking putts.

3-4. Randomly place 10 balls around a cup at various distances of more than 15 feet. Deliberately read each putt and describe out loud to a partner or the instructor which way it will break, how much it will break, and how hard you need to hit the putt. If your partner does not agree with you, ask him or her to explain his or her observations. Once you both agree, assume the proper stance and hit the putt.

If you experience difficulty with these readiness drills, refer to the **Performance Cues** for putting and for reading putts and review each cue as presented. If you still have difficulty, ask your course instructor to assist you in applying these techniques.

CRITERION TASKS FOR BREAKING PUTTS

Find a place on the putting practice area with an open cup to aim for. Make sure that there is some break in the putts you will be attempting. More than one student can be aiming at the same cup, so you will likely have to share a cup. When the distance increases, you will need to pay attention to other students practicing in front of you. Do not attempt to make the mastery criterion right away for each new task. Hit putts until you become consistent, and then try to reach the mastery criterion.

CRITERION TASK 3-5

Self-Checked

1. *Distance from hole:* 15 feet
2. *Target:* Holed putt, or stop within 2 feet of hole (any direction)
3. *Criterion:* Inside target 6 of 10 putts, 3 times

Practice this task in blocks of 10 putts. Record the number of successful putts in each block on the **Personal Recording Form**. When three block scores reach or exceed 6 (does not have to be consecutive blocks), initial and date in the space provided.

Personal Recording Form									
Block 1	Block 2	Block 3	Block 4	Block 5	Block 6	Block 7	Block 8	Block 9	Block 10
__/10	__/10	__/10	__/10	__/10	__/10	__/10	__/10	__/10	__/10

Your initials _____ Date completed _____

CRITERION TASK 3-6

Instructor-Checked

1. *Distance from hole:* 30-35 feet
2. *Target:* Holed putt, or stop within 6 feet of hole (any direction)
3. *Criterion:* Inside target 5 of 10 putts, 3 times

Practice this task in blocks of 10 putts. Record the number of successful putts for each block on the **Personal Recording Form.** When your block scores regularly approach or exceed 5 out of 10, ask your instructor to observe and witness your reaching of criterion. When your instructor has observed three successful blocks, he or she will initial and date in the space provided.

Personal Recording Form									
Block 1	Block 2	Block 3	Block 4	Block 5	Block 6	Block 7	Block 8	Block 9	Block 10
___/10	___/10	___/10	___/10	___/10	___/10	___/10	___/10	___/10	___/10

Instructor's initials _____   Date completed _____

MODULE 4

COMPLETE GOLF SWING FOR BEGINNERS

INTRODUCTION

There are many theories about the best way to hit a golf ball for distance, accuracy, and consistency. What makes this confusing is that some theories are completely opposite from others so not all of them can be correct! There are also many ways to teach (and learn) the golf swing. Again, some ways are totally opposite from others, so not all of them can be correct. Some teachers view the golf swing as a very complex chain of fine and powerful movements that must be performed to exact specifications every time to build consistency. Other teachers view the golf swing as less technical, based more on timing, comfort, and rhythm. The approach in PSIS golf is somewhere between these two extremes. You will develop your skill by learning the essential parts of the golf swing, but not with a high reliance on a large number of technical terms. The objective is to teach you how to make a smooth, efficient, and correct swing for every shot covered in this course. However, these characteristics are developed at the beginner level so that you can progress to a place that will allow you to confidently play the game, but knowing that you still have lots of room to develop further.

PSIS golf also uses a unique green-to-tee plan in which the smallest swing (the putt) comes first, followed by progressively longer shots, leading to hitting tee shots with wood clubs. Each new swing technique builds on what you have learned to do with earlier shots, giving you a familiar base at all times.

There is no single *correct* way to swing the golf club; neither is there just *one* type of swing that can be used for all shots. Putting involves a setup and swing that are different from all other shots, so it was introduced on its own and learned first. Different from putting, there are some *swing basics* that all beginners should learn and follow to achieve consistent results and progressively lower scores. This section discusses some key performance cues that can be applied to nearly every shot in golf (except putting). Be aware that, from time to time, your instructor will alert you to exceptions to these basics, and provide you with the proper alternatives.

INSTRUCTOR DEMONSTRATION

Your course instructor will provide you with an explanation and demonstration of the key performance cues for the complete golf swing. If you have questions, be sure to ask them before proceeding to the individualized task sequence. Refer to Photos 4.1A through G as your instructor explains and demonstrates each performance cue and presents the learning tips.

Photo 4.1A
Set up and stance

COMPLETE GOLF SWING FOR BEGINNERS 47

Photo 4.1B
Take-away (start of backswing)

Photo 4.1C
Top of backswing

48 MODULE 4

Photo 4.1D
Beginning of descent

Photo 4.1E
Contact point

COMPLETE GOLF SWING FOR BEGINNERS **49**

Photo 4.1F
Frontswing

Photo 4.1G
Follow-through

SET UP AND PERFORMANCE CUES

1. **Assume the correct setup position.** All shots start with the proper grip, stance, aiming line, ball positioning, and hand positioning. The correct techniques for these components change for many shots and are explained in more detail in later modules.
2. **Keep your head still and down.** This is often called golf's "only unbreakable rule" because it is impossible to hit the ball properly if you can't see it! Once you have made your setup, focus on the back of the ball, and keep your head down and still for the entire swing. Lifting your head only at the very end of your follow-through.
3. **Keep your front arm straight on the backswing and frontswing.** Think of your front arm as an extension of the club's shaft, which is also straight. Keep your front arm very straight on the backswing and frontswing. Bend it only at the end of your follow-through.
4. **Keep your wrists firm.** A firm wrist means that your hands grip the club so that the clubhead does not wobble during the swing (especially at the top of the backswing). This provides the fine degree of control needed to make consistently good shots.
5. **Shift your weight with the clubhead.** Your weight should be equally distributed over both feet during the setup. As the clubhead moves back in your backswing, gently shift some of your weight over your back leg. Shift your weight forward as the clubhead moves in that direction until your weight is almost entirely over your front leg as the follow-through is completed.
6. **Always follow through.** The golf swing is not complete when the ball leaves the club. It is complete when you have made the proper follow-through called for on each shot. The length of follow-through is related to the length of the backswing; they should be similar to promote an even swing tempo.
7. **Swing on a nearly upright plane.** The swing plane for the golf swing is nearly upright. This means it approaches being vertical to the ground, but is not straight up and down.
8. **Adjust your swing length for different distances.** For many golf shots, the best way to hit the ball longer is to *swing longer*, not harder! This means adjusting your swing to gain more momentum with a longer swing arc, not swinging harder at the ball. Swinging harder might give you longer distance, but it will likely also result in greatly reduced control.

LEARNING TIPS

1. **Develop and use a preshot routine.** Consistency is key for successful golf. Take your time on every shot and develop a preshot routine that is comfortable for you and USE IT EVERY TIME. It is a good idea to use this routine even on the practice tee.
2. **Always have an objective.** It is a good idea to ask yourself on every shot, "What do I want this shot to do? How far should it go? How high should it go?" These questions provide you with information for determining club selection, aiming line, and landing area.
3. **Always check your grip and setup.** You might be surprised to learn that most errant shots are a result of an improper grip and setup, not an improper swing. Essentially, the setup describes how you want everything to look when the club is making contact with the ball. If this "picture" is not correct, your chances of making a good shot are greatly reduced.
4. **Use a smooth swing tempo.** One secret to a good golf swing is having an easy, smooth tempo over the entire swing path. This means that the club is drawn backward carefully and slowly and then brought forward with only a slight increase in speed as contact is about to be made. Jerky movements or an uneven tempo produce erratic shots.
5. **Strive for consistency.** The best golfers develop consistent patterns in shot making, so when they have a known distance to the target, they have a better chance of making the correct club selection and executing a swing that will go the needed distance.
6. **Practice smart.** Many beginners are tempted to hit as many practice shots as they can in a given time, thinking that since "more is better" they will improve faster. This is not the case. Golf is a precision game, so you must be able to practice at a relaxed pace, using your preshot routine on every shot, checking and double-checking your setup, and not hitting a ball until you are ready.

READINESS DRILLS

4-1. Get a short iron (8- or 9-iron or pitching wedge), and find a place on the practice area. Without hitting balls at this time, complete 100 practice swings in slow motion, checking your performance cues at every step of the way. Be sure to use your preshot routine on every swing.

4-2. Using the same club and with balls placed on tees, complete 75 practice shots at half-speed. Be sure to use your preshot routine on every shot. Your objective is to get the ball up in the air consistently. Do not be concerned with distance or accuracy at this time.

4-3. Using the same club and with balls placed on tees, complete 75 practice shots at full speed, but under control. Be sure to use your preshot routine on every shot. Your objective is to get the ball up in the air consistently. Do not be concerned with distance or accuracy at this time.

MODULE 5

AROUND THE GREEN

INTRODUCTION

Most beginning players cannot land the ball directly on the green consistently from long distances. Typically, they find themselves with a short shot from just off the putting area, so they cannot putt yet. And often, obstacles such as sand traps must be considered. To get the ball on the green and near the hole for putting, you can use one of two swing techniques: either a **chip swing** or a **pitch swing**. Each swing is described separately, but remember that the purpose of both shots is to get the ball near enough to the hole to ensure making your first putt. In golf, this is called "getting up and down in two" (one chip or pitch and one putt). It is an important skill for beginners who have not yet mastered the ability to land their ball on the green from long distances.

CHIPPING

The **chip swing**, or *chipping*, is used when your ball is near the edge of the green and must roll a long distance to reach the hole. The chipping stroke produces a shot with little loft and more roll, making it look like a putt once it hits the green. Since it looks very much like the putt, players usually have more control when chipping (over pitching), so it is desirable to use the chip swing if possible.

MODULE 5

INSTRUCTOR DEMONSTRATION

Your course instructor will provide you with an explanation and demonstration of the key performance cues for the chipping swing. If you have questions, be sure to ask them before proceeding to the individualized task sequence. Refer to Photos 5.1A through E as your instructor explains and demonstrates each performance cue and presents the learning tips.

Photo 5.1A
Set up and stance

AROUND THE GREEN 55

Photo 5.1B
Top of backswing

Photo 5.1C
Contact point

56 MODULE 5

Photo 5.1D
Frontswing

Photo 5.1E
follow-through

SET UP AND PERFORMANCE CUES

1. **Club choice:** 5- or 7-iron
2. **Grip:** Interlocked or overlapped
3. **Stance:** Square or *slightly* open, knees bent and stiff (not locked)
4. **Ball placement:** On midline
5. **Hands alignment:** Choked down on the club and slightly in front of midline
6. **Clubface:** Square to aiming line
7. **Aiming line:** Similar to breaking putt (remember to determine and account for break after the ball hits the green)
8. **Swing path:** Straight back and forth on aiming line with pendulum (putting) motion
9. **Swing length:** One-quarter swing
10. **Follow-through:** Equal length as backswing, maintain even clubhead speed until completed; keep hands low on follow-through

COMPREHENSION TASK

Find a partner and demonstrate to each other the proper performance cues for the chip swing *without hitting the ball*. Be sure to provide feedback to each other for correct and incorrect performance cues until both of you can correctly execute this stroke.

LEARNING TIPS

1. Make the chip swing identical to the putting swing (review if necessary). Think of chipping simply as "putting from off the green" with a different club.
2. Plan for one-third of the distance in flight and two-thirds from roll. Aim for a spot about one-third of the distance from your ball to the cup.
3. Square stance + square clubface + hands in front = reduced loft, more roll.
4. Swing to hit the grass below the ball, not the ball itself.
5. It is essential that you keep your head down at all times.
6. Remember that the ball will roll once on the green, so consider break before you determine your aiming line.

MODULE 5

READINESS DRILL

5-1. Gather about 10 balls and drop them about 5 feet from the edge of the putting green practice area. Using your preshot routine and the proper setup for chipping, hit 50 chip shots. At this time your goals should be to get the ball in the air with a low loft consistently and to hit the ball straight. Do not be concerned with distance to begin with.

If you experience difficulty with the readiness drill, refer to the **Performance Cues** and review each cue as presented. If you still have difficulty, contact your course instructor to assist you in applying these techniques.

Common Errors and Their Correction

Error	Correction
Punching the ball (hitting it hard with no follow-through). This results in erratic distance: very short one time, very long the next.	1. Make backswing and follow-through the same length and (even) speed. 2. Have sure your hands maintain their momentum well past contact with the ball.
Peeking (lifting your head before follow-through is complete). This results in inconsistent errors; sometimes way right, sometimes way left, sometimes topping the ball, making it dribble onto the green.	Complete follow-through, count 1... 2, then lift head.
Lifting (trying to help the club lift the ball off the ground). This results in higher loft and reduced control.	Don't aim to hit the ball; try to hit the *grass it sits on*. Let the club do the work.
Overswing (swinging too hard). This results in a shot that flies or rolls far past the hole.	Make a softer swing, or a shorter swing. Remember, the ball will roll after it lands on the green.
Forgetting the basics (not making the chip swing like that for a putt). This results in a variety of errors.	Remember, you already know how to putt, so make the chip swing the same as a putt swing. Build on what you have already learned!

CRITERION TASK 5-1

Chipping: Self-Checked

1. *Place the ball:* 5 feet off the green, 25 feet from the cup
2. *Target:* Stop the ball within 6 feet of the cup (any direction)
3. *Criterion:* Inside target 5 of 10 chips, 3 times

Practice this task in blocks of 10 shots. Record the number of successful shots in each block on the **Personal Recording Form**. When three block scores reach or exceed 6 (does not have to be consecutive blocks), initial and date in the space provided.

Personal Recording Form									
Block 1	Block 2	Block 3	Block 4	Block 5	Block 6	Block 7	Block 8	Block 9	Block 10
___/10	___/10	___/10	___/10	___/10	___/10	___/10	___/10	___/10	___/10

Your initials _____ Date completed _____

CRITERION TASK 5-2

Chipping: Instructor-Checked

1. *Place the ball:* 10 feet off the green, 40 feet from the cup
2. *Target:* Stop the ball within 6 feet of the cup (any direction)
3. *Criterion:* Inside target 6 of 10 chips, 3 times

Practice this task in blocks of 10 shots. Record the number of successful shots for each block on the **Personal Recording Form.** When your block scores regularly approach or exceed 6 out of 10, ask your instructor to observe and witness your reaching of criterion. When your instructor has observed three successful blocks, he or she will initial and date in the space provided.

Personal Recording Form									
Block 1	Block 2	Block 3	Block 4	Block 5	Block 6	Block 7	Block 8	Block 9	Block 10
__/10	__/10	__/10	__/10	__/10	__/10	__/10	__/10	__/10	__/10

Instructor's initials _____   Date completed _____

PITCHING

INTRODUCTION

Although most players have more control with the chip swing, it will not always happen that your landing spot for a chip shot is on the green, giving you a controlled roll. At times your shot must have *more loft* to clear obstacles between your ball and the green, like a sand trap, or *less roll* to stay near the cup. In these instances, you will need to use the **pitch swing** or pitch shot to get the ball on the green and near the cup in order to get "up and down in two." The pitch shot calls for a very different technique from chipping. As you recall, the chip shot produces less loft and more roll. The pitch shot is just the opposite. You want high loft with little roll once the ball hits the green.

INSTRUCTOR DEMONSTRATION

Your course instructor will provide you with an explanation and demonstration of the key performance cues for the pitch swing. If you have questions, be sure to ask them before proceeding to the individualized task sequence. Refer to Photos 5.2A through E as your instructor explains and demonstrates each performance cue and presents the learning tips.

Photo 5.2A
Setup and stance

Photo 5.2B
Top of backswing

Photo 5.2C
Contact point

AROUND THE GREEN 63

Photo 5.2D
Frontswing

Photo 5.2E
Follow-through.

SETUP AND PERFORMANCE CUES

1. **Club Selection:** 9-iron or pitching wedge
2. **Grip:** Interlocked or overlapped
3. **Stance:** Slightly open, knees slightly bent (but not locked)
4. **Ball placement:** On midline
5. **Hands alignment:** Choked down on club, slightly in front of midline
6. **Clubface:** Slightly open
7. **Aiming line:** Similar to breaking putt (remember to determine and account for break after the ball hits the green)
8. **Swing path:** Straight back and forth on aiming line with pendulum (putting) motion
9. **Swing length:** One-quarter to one-half, depending on needed loft and distance
10. **Follow-through:** Equal length as backswing, maintain even clubhead speed until completed; important to finish with *hands high*

COMPREHENSION TASK

Find a partner and demonstrate to each other the proper performance cues for the pitch swing *without hitting the ball*. Be sure to provide feedback to each other for correct and incorrect performance cues until both of you can correctly execute this stroke.

LEARNING TIPS

1. The pitch shot will give you two-thirds of the distance in ball flight and one-third in roll. So determine the correct landing spot before you set up over the ball.
2. Three major factors increase the amount of loft: using a lofted club, keeping the clubface open, and (most importantly) making a complete follow-through.
3. Keep the putting basics intact and your head DOWN!
4. Use the *swing triangle*, unlocking your wrists only after making contact with the ball (to increase follow-through).
5. Gradually shift your weight with the head of the club to your back leg on backswing and then to your front leg on downswing and follow-through.

READINESS DRILL

5-2. Gather some golf balls and drop them about 10 feet from the edge of the putting green practice area. Using your preshot routine and the proper setup for pitching, hit 50 pitch shots. At this time your goals should be to get the ball in the air with loft consistently and to hit the ball straight. Do not be concerned with distance to begin with.

If you experience difficulty with the readiness drill, refer to the **Performance Cues** and review each cue as presented. If you still have difficulty, contact your course instructor to assist you in applying these techniques.

Common Errors and Their Correction

Error	Correction
Punching the ball (fast swing with no follow-through). This results in low loft and erratic distance: very short one time, very long the next.	1. Make backswing and follow-through the same length and (even) speed. 2. Finish with hands high, about eye level.
Peeking (lifting your head before follow-through is complete). This results in inconsistent errors; sometimes way right, sometimes way left, sometimes topping the ball, causing it to dribble onto the green.	Complete follow-through, count 1... 2, then lift head.
Lifting (trying to help the club lift the ball off the ground). This results in excessive loft and reduced control.	Don't aim for the ball; try to hit the *grass it sits on*. And let the club do the work.
Overswing (swinging too hard). This results in a shot that flies or rolls far past the hole.	Make a softer swing, or a shorter swing. Remember, the ball will roll after it lands on the green.
Loose wrists (excessive flexing of the wrists). Results in greatly reduced control.	Keep wrists flexed on backswing and follow-through, but **firm** on the front swing.

CRITERION TASKS FOR PITCHING

Find a place on the fringe of the practice area with an open cup to aim for. More than one student can be aiming at the same cup, so you will likely have to share a cup. When the distance increases, you will need to pay attention to other students practicing in front of you. Do not attempt to make the mastery criterion right away for each new task. Hit pitches until you become consistent, and then try to reach the mastery criterion.

CRITERION TASK 5-3

Self-Checked

1. *Place your ball:* 5 feet off the green, 15 feet from the cup
2. *Target:* Stop the ball within 6 feet of the cup (any direction)
3. *Criterion:* Inside target 6 of 10 pitches, 3 times

Practice this task in blocks of 10 shots. Record the number of successful shots in each block on the **Personal Recording Form**. When three block scores reach or exceed 6 (does not have to be consecutive blocks), initial and date in the space provided.

Personal Recording Form									
Block 1	Block 2	Block 3	Block 4	Block 5	Block 6	Block 7	Block 8	Block 9	Block 10
___/10	___/10	___/10	___/10	___/10	___/10	___/10	___/10	___/10	___/10

Your initials _____   Date completed _____

CRITERION TASK 5-4

Self-Checked

1. *Place your ball:* 10 feet off the green, 35 feet from the cup
2. *Target:* Stop the ball within 8 feet of the cup (any direction)
3. *Criterion:* Inside target 5 of 10 pitches, 3 times

Practice this task in blocks of 10 shots. Record the number of successful shots in each block on the **Personal Recording Form**. When three block scores reach or exceed 5 (does not have to be consecutive blocks), initial and date in the space provided.

Personal Recording Form									
Block 1	Block 2	Block 3	Block 4	Block 5	Block 6	Block 7	Block 8	Block 9	Block 10
__/10	__/10	__/10	__/10	__/10	__/10	__/10	__/10	__/10	__/10

Your initials _____   Date completed _____

CRITERION TASK 5-5

Instructor-Checked

1. *Place your ball:* 10 yards off the green, 25 yards from the cup
2. *Target:* Stop within 10 feet of the cup (any direction)
3. *Criterion:* Inside target 5 of 10 pitches, 2 times

Practice this task in blocks of 10 shots. Record the number of successful shots for each block on the **Personal Recording Form**. When your block scores regularly approach or exceed 5 out of 10, ask your instructor to observe and witness your reaching of criterion. When your instructor has observed two successful blocks, he or she will initial and date in the space provided.

Personal Recording Form									
Block 1	Block 2	Block 3	Block 4	Block 5	Block 6	Block 7	Block 8	Block 9	Block 10
__/10	__/10	__/10	__/10	__/10	__/10	__/10	__/10	__/10	__/10

Instructor's initials _____   Date completed _____

MODULE 6

APPROACH SHOTS WITH IRONS

INTRODUCTION

Approach shots are used to land your ball on the green from a distance that is too long for chipping or pitching. The purpose of the approach shot is to stop the ball safely on the putting green with a good chance to finish the hole with no more than two putts. Most approach shots call for the use of shorter clubs with higher loft. In most instances, the more loft on the shot, the less the ball will roll after it hits the green, so the object is to aim for the pin (the flagstick in the cup). The best target for most approach shots is the green itself. Novice players should not be overly concerned with trying to get their approach shots to stop near the cup; for now, stopping the ball on the green is more than sufficient.

INSTRUCTOR DEMONSTRATION

Your course instructor will provide you with an explanation and demonstration of the key setup and performance cues for hitting approach shots, including club selection. Refer to Photos 6.1A through G for pictures of the full golf swing that you learned in Module 4. The club you select depends on the distance you have to the green, relative to your own personal hitting power. In general, you will want to select the club that allows you to reach the needed distance with the most loft, producing less roll once the ball hits the green. If you have questions, be sure to ask them before proceeding to the individualized task sequence.

MODULE 6

Photo 6.1A
Setup and stance

Photo 6.B
Take-away (start of backswing)

APPROACH SHOTS WITH IRONS   **71**

Photo 6.1C
Top of backswing

Photo 6.1D
Beginning of descent

72   MODULE 6

Photo 6.1E
Contact point

Photo 6.1F
Frontswing

APPROACH SHOTS WITH IRONS **73**

Photo 6.1G
Follow-through

SET UP AND PERFORMANCE CUES

1. **Club choice:** Determined by distance to target and individual hitting length; shorter hitters use 7-iron (50 yards) to wooded club (150 yards); longer hitters use sand wedge (50 yards) to 7-iron (150 yards)
2. **Grip:** Interlocked or overlapped
3. **Stance:** Square, bend slightly at knees (but keep knees flexible)
4. **Ball placement:** *Slightly* to the front, or on mid-line
5. **Hands alignment:** On midline, slightly below your belt buckle
6. **Clubface:** Square to aiming line
7. **Aiming line:** To middle of the green or other target area
8. **Swing path:** Slightly inside on backswing, on aiming line for frontswing, slightly inside on follow-through
9. **Swing Length:** Three-quarters to full, depending on distance and selected club
10. **Follow-through:** Equal length as backswing, maintain even clubhead speed until completed; important to stay on swing path and finish with *hands high*

COMPREHENSION TASK

Find a partner and demonstrate to each other the proper performance cues for the approach shot swing using a 4-, 5-, or 6-iron and *without hitting the ball*. Be sure to provide feedback to each other for correct and incorrect performance cues until both of you can correctly execute this stroke.

LEARNING TIPS

1. Do not be concerned about which club you use to hit the ball a given distance. *Select the one **you** need to reach the target with the most loft.*
2. Keep your head down at all times (until follow-through is complete).
3. Flex your wrists "at the top", but keep your grip firm on the downswing.
4. Keep the basics intact. This is not a **different** swing than pitching, only a **longer** one!
5. Place the ball on a tee if you initially have difficulty getting loft on the ball. However, do not depend on the tee for too long.
6. When practicing, be sure your ball rests on some grass and level ground. It is almost impossible to get loft off bare ground or if the ball sits in a depression.
7. Be sure to have a target in mind and use your preshot routine on every practice attempt. Avoid the habit of just hitting one ball after another.

READINESS DRILL

6-1. Using a 100-yard distance, experiment with several clubs to determine which allows you to reach this distance with the most loft. Hit with each club about 20 times or until you can tell if it is too long or too short for this distance. Use a tee if necessary, since the tee will not give you greater distance—only greater loft. Do not be concerned with accuracy at this point. You can then use this as your reference distance and club as you begin the approach shot sequence Remember, use your preshot routine on every practice shot!

If you experience difficulty with the readiness drill, refer to the **Performance Cues** and review each cue as presented. If you still have difficulty, contact your course instructor to assist you in applying these techniques.

Common Errors and Their Correction

Error	**Correction**
Slicing (the ball curves severely away from your target on the opposite side of your aiming line; see Illustrations 6.1 and 6.2)	1. Usually caused by opening the clubface too much at contact. 2. Check grip and alignment of feet and hands. 3. Keep your head down all the way through the swing. 4. Follow through, count 1... 2, then lift head.
Hooking (the ball curves severely away from your target on your side of the aiming line; see Illustrations 6.1 and 6.2)	1. Usually caused by closing the clubface too much at contact. 2. Check grip and alignment of feet and hands. 3. Do not "roll" your top hand in your grip after contact. 4. Be sure your weight does not come forward too quickly on the frontswing.
Pulling (the ball goes immediately to your side of the aiming line, with no curve.	1. Usually caused by an *outside-in* swing path. 2. Keep club on (not outside) aiming line on backswing.
Pushing (the ball goes immediately away from your side of the aiming line, with no curve.	1. Usually caused by an *inside-out* swing path. 2. Keep club on (not inside) aiming line on backswing.
No loft on ball.	1. Check grip, stance, and ball alignment and make sure club face is not closed. 2. Follow through on proper swing path. 3. Swing harder!
Inconsistent shots, no pattern to the problem.	1. Remember your preshot routine and use it. 2. Check grip, stance, and alignment cues before every shot. 3. Keep eyes on ball from address through contact. 4. Keep head down until follow-through is complete.

MODULE 6

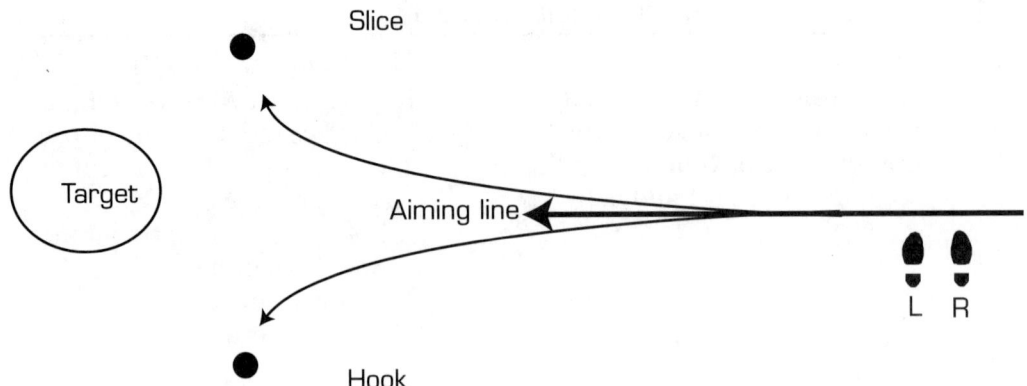

Illustration 6.1
Right hander's slice and hook patterns

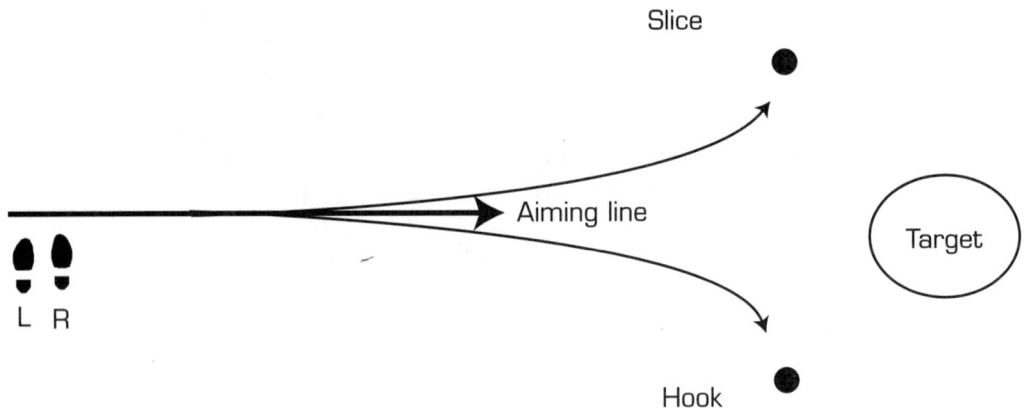

Illustration 6.2
Left hander's slice and hook patterns

CRITERION TASKS FOR APPROACH SHOTS

Practice note: As you improve your swing and ball contact, you will increase the distance and loft you get with each club. When you move to a longer practice distance, try the new distance with the club you just used. If you are making good contact, but can't reach the new distance, then select a longer club. Your instructor will have measured and marked several distances for this part of the PSIS skill sequence. The target for these shots stays the same, a marked area about the size of a large golf green. The only things that change in this progression are the distance you stand from the target area and the club selection for each distance.

APPROACH SHOTS WITH IRONS

CRITERION TASK 6-1

Self-Checked

1. *Distance:* 60 yards from center of target
2. *Target:* Hit target on the fly or with no more than a short roll
3. *Criterion:* 5 of 10 shots on target, 2 times

Practice this task in blocks of 10 shots. Record the number of successful shots in each block on the **Personal Recording Form**. When three block scores reach or exceed 5 (does not have to be consecutive blocks), initial and date in the space provided.

Personal Recording Form									
Block 1	Block 2	Block 3	Block 4	Block 5	Block 6	Block 7	Block 8	Block 9	Block 10
___/10	___/10	___/10	___/10	___/10	___/10	___/10	___/10	___/10	___/10

Your initials _____   Date completed _____

CRITERION TASK 6-2

Self-Checked

1. *Distance:* 90 to 100 yards from center of target
2. *Target:* Longer hitters: Marked target on the fly
   Shorter hitters: Marked target on the fly or with no more than 20 yards of roll
3. *Criterion:* 5 of 10 shots on target, 3 times

Practice this task in blocks of 10 shots. Record the number of successful shots in each block on the **Personal Recording Form**. When three block scores reach or exceed 5 (does not have to be consecutive blocks), initial and date in the space provided.

Personal Recording Form									
Block 1	Block 2	Block 3	Block 4	Block 5	Block 6	Block 7	Block 8	Block 9	Block 10
___/10	___/10	___/10	___/10	___/10	___/10	___/10	___/10	___/10	___/10

Your initials _____   Date completed _____

CRITERION TASK 6-3

Self-Checked

1. *Distance:* 120 to 130 yards from center of target
2. *Target:* Longer hitters: Marked target on the fly
   Shorter hitters: Marked target on the fly or with no more than 20 yards of roll
3. *Criterion:* 5 of 10 shots on target, 3 times

Practice this task in blocks of 10 shots. Record the number of successful shots in each block on the **Personal Recording Form**. When three block scores reach or exceed 5 (does not have to be consecutive blocks), initial and date in the space provided.

Personal Recording Form									
Block 1	Block 2	Block 3	Block 4	Block 5	Block 6	Block 7	Block 8	Block 9	Block 10
___/10	___/10	___/10	___/10	___/10	___/10	___/10	___/10	___/10	___/10

Your initials _____ Date completed _____

CRITERION TASK 6-4

Instructor-Checked

1. *Distance:* 150 to 160 yards from the center of the target
2. *Target:* Longer hitters: Marked target on the fly
   Shorter hitters: Marked target on the fly or with no more than 20 yards of roll
3. *Criterion:* Inside target 5 of 10 shots, 2 times

Practice this task in blocks of 10 shots. Record the number of successful shots for each block on the **Personal Recording Form**. When your block scores regularly approach or exceed 5 out of 10, ask your instructor to observe and witness your reaching of criterion. When your instructor has observed two successful blocks, he or she will initial and date in the space provided.

Personal Recording Form									
Block 1	Block 2	Block 3	Block 4	Block 5	Block 6	Block 7	Block 8	Block 9	Block 10
__/10	__/10	__/10	__/10	__/10	__/10	__/10	__/10	__/10	__/10

Instructor's initials _____   Date completed _____

CRITERION TASK 6-5 (OPTIONAL)

Self-Checked

1. *Distance:* 170 to 180 yards from the center of the target
2. *Target:* Longer hitters: Marked target on the fly
   Shorter hitters: Marked target on the fly or with no more than 20 yards of roll
3. *Criterion:* Inside target 4 of 10 shots, 2 times

Practice this task in blocks of 10 shots. Record the number of successful shots for each block on the **Personal Recording Form**. When you are successful on four or more attempts in two blocks (does not have to be consecutive), initial and date in the space provided.

Personal Recording Form									
Block 1	Block 2	Block 3	Block 4	Block 5	Block 6	Block 7	Block 8	Block 9	Block 10
__/10	__/10	__/10	__/10	__/10	__/10	__/10	__/10	__/10	__/10

Your initials _____   Date completed _____

MODULE 7

STARTING THE HOLE: TEE SHOTS

INTRODUCTION

Every hole of golf begins from the teeing area, as defined in the rules. It is the only spot from which you are allowed to place your ball on a tee for striking; therefore, these are called **tee shots**. You can legally use any club when hitting a teed ball, but most golf holes will call for the use of a wood club, usually the **driver**. The purpose of the tee shot is to get maximum distance while landing the ball on the **fairway**. However, for beginning players, distance is much less important than accuracy, so work to hit your tee shots accurately to the fairway.

Although you can legally use any club for your tee shot, nearly all tee shots call for the use of a wood (metal), and so only those are discussed here. When you choose to use an iron from the tee, simply keep in mind all the performance cues you have already learned for *approach shots*.

MODULE 7

INSTRUCTOR DEMONSTRATION

Your course instructor will provide you with an explanation and demonstration of the key performance cues for tee shots. If you have questions, be sure to ask them before proceeding to the individualized task sequence. Refer to Photos 7.1A through I as your instructor explains and demonstrates each performance cue and presents the learning tips.

Photo 7.1A
Setup and stance, front view

STARTING THE HOLE: TEE SHOTS **85**

Photo 7.1B
Setup and stance, view toward target

Photo 7.1C
Take-back

MODULE 7

Photo 7.1D
Near top of backswing

Photo 7.1E
Top of backswing

STARTING THE HOLE: TEE SHOTS 87

Photo 7.1F
Frontswing descent

Photo 7.1G
Contact point

MODULE 7

Photo 7.1H
Frontswing (start of follow-through)

Photo 7.1I
Follow-through

SET UP AND PERFORMANCE CUES

1. **Club choice:** Driver, 2-wood, 3-wood, 4-wood or long iron. Select the one with which you hit the most accurately, not the longest distance
2. **Grip:** Interlocked or overlapped
3. **Stance:** Square, bend slightly at knees (but keep knees flexible)
4. **Ball placement:** Just behind the heel of the front foot
5. **Teeing height:** Tee the ball between 1 and 1 1/2 inches off the ground; loft will increase with teeing height
6. **Hands alignment:** Slightly in front of midline, comfortable reach away, slightly below your belt buckle
7. **Clubface:** Square to aiming line
8. **Aiming line:** To middle of the fairway (or other desired landing area)
9. **Swing path:** Slightly inside aiming line on backswing, on aiming line for frontswing, slightly inside aiming line on follow-through
10. **Swing length:** Full
11. **Follow-through:** Equal length as backswing, maintain even clubhead speed until completed; important to stay on swing path and finish with hands high.

COMPREHENSION TASK

Find a partner and demonstrate to each other the proper performance cues for the tee shot swing with a wood club and *without hitting the ball*. Be sure to provide feedback to each other for correct and incorrect performance cues until both of you can correctly execute this stroke.

LEARNING TIPS

1. Wood clubs are more difficult to hit accurately because they are longer and heavier than irons. Woods are also designed for longer distance, so you can take advantage of this by swinging smoothly, with an even tempo, and concentrating hard to execute all the proper setup and swing cues. As you will learn, mistakes made when using wood clubs tend to be

more exaggerated (going farther off line and into more trouble), but well-struck tee shots will greatly increase your chances of success on each hole.
2. Remember to use your preshot routine and the proper setup cues
3. Keep your wrists firm on the backswing. The extra weight of the clubhead can cause it to wobble at the top which can produce very inconsistent tee shots.
4. Swing easy and in control. It is better to be in the fairway and short than off the fairway or out of bounds and long. Let the club do the work for you.
5. Keep your head down at all times, until follow-through is complete.
6. Shift your weight with the travel of the club: to your back foot on the backswing, then to your front foot on front swing and follow-through.
7. Keep your front arm straight from alignment to follow-through. Think of your front arm and the clubshaft as one *long* clubshaft.

READINESS DRILL

7-1. Your instructor will mark out a practice area for tee shots. Experiment with each of the listed clubs by hitting about 50 shots with each. Make notes in the following table of the usual distance, accuracy, and tendencies you have with each of the different clubs. **Remember, the "usual" distance does not mean the longest distance you achieved with each club; it is your average distance.**

If you experience difficulty with the readiness drill, refer to the **Performance Cues**

Club	My usual distance	Accuracy (low, high)	Tendency (slice, hook, straight)
Driver			
3-Wood			
5-Wood			
Other			

and review each cue as presented. If you still have difficulty, contact your course instructor to assist you in applying these techniques.

Common Errors and Their Correction

Error	Correction
Slicing (the ball curves severely away from your target on the opposite side of your aiming line).	1. Usually caused by opening the clubface too much at contact. 2. Check grip and alignment of feet and hands. 3. Keep your head down all the way through the stroke. 4. Follow through, count 1... 2, then lift head.
Hooking (the ball curves severely away from your target on your side of the aiming line).	1. Usually caused by closing the clubface too much at contact. 2. Check grip and alignment of feet and hands. 3. Do not "roll" your top hand in your grip after contact. 4. Be sure your weight does not come forward too quickly on the frontswing.
Pulling (the ball goes immediately to your side of the aiming line, with no curve).	1. Usually caused by an *outside-in* swing path. 2. Keep club on (not outside) aiming line on backswing.
Pushing (the ball goes immediately away from your side of the aiming line, with no curve).	1. Usually caused by an *inside-out* swing path. 2. Keep club on (not inside) aiming line on.backswing.
Pop fly shots (very high with little distance).	1. Tee the ball lower. 2. Keep head down and hands low right after contact.

Common Errors and Their Correction (continued)

Error

No loft on ball.

Correction

1. Check grip, stance and ball alignment and make sure club face is not closed.
2. Follow through on proper swing path.
3. Swing harder!

Error

Inconsistent shots, no pattern to the problem.

Correction

1. Remember your preshot routine and use it.
2. Check grip, stance, and alignment cues before every shot.
3. Keep eyes on ball from address through contact.
4. Keep head down until follow-through is complete.

CRITERION TASK 7-1

Tee Shots: Instructor-Checked

1. From the chart you made for the Readiness Drill, select the club with which you hit the most accurately.
2. Note the usual distance you hit the ball with this club.
3. Select your personal distance and accuracy target from Illustration 7.1 and practice hitting balls to this target.

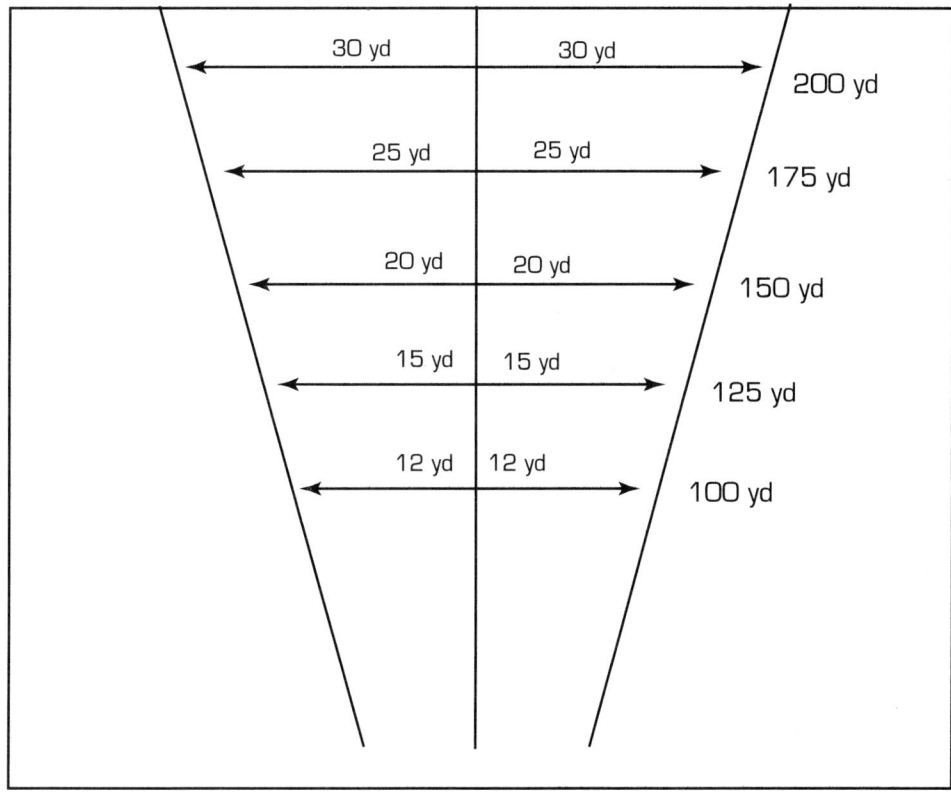

Illustration 7.1
Distance and accuracy targets for tee shots

MODULE 7

The criterion for this task is to hit 5 of 10 shots that go past your assigned distance (including roll) *and* within your indicated target width area (2 times, which do not have to be consecutive).

Practice your tee shots in blocks of 10, trying to reach both your distance and accuracy criterion on each shot. Record the number of successful shots for each block on the **Personal Recording Form**. When your block scores regularly approach or exceed 5 out of 10, ask your instructor to observe and witness your mastery attempt. When your instructor has observed two successful blocks, he or she will initial and date in the space provided.

Personal Recording Form									
Block 1	Block 2	Block 3	Block 4	Block 5	Block 6	Block 7	Block 8	Block 9	Block 10
__/10	__/10	__/10	__/10	__/10	__/10	__/10	__/10	__/10	__/10

Instructor's initials _____   Date completed _____

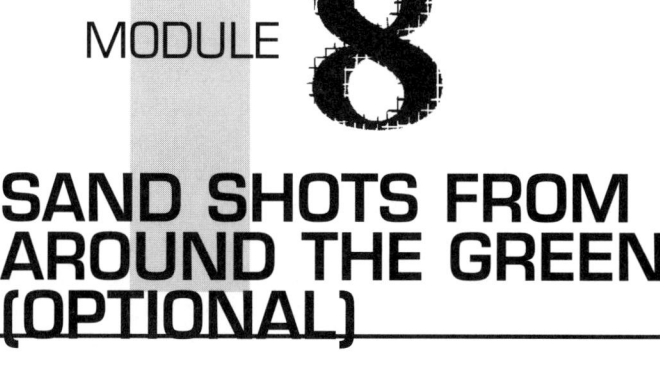

MODULE 8
SAND SHOTS FROM AROUND THE GREEN (OPTIONAL)

INTRODUCTION

This is an optional task sequence in your PSIS golf course. Check with your instructor to see if this sequence is part of his or her planned coverage for your course. If not, you can read this module and complete it on your own outside class time.

To make the game more challenging, many putting greens are "protected" with sand traps. A green can have one or more sand traps around it, often located in places that "collect" the results of errant approach shots. There is no penalty in the rules for landing in a sand trap, but hitting out of the sand reduces the player's control and often results in an extra shot to get the ball into the cup, thus providing a practical penalty of sorts if the player cannot negotiate the sand properly.

The difficulty in playing out of a sand trap comes in several ways. First, the ball can settle into the sand, making it difficult to get loft on the ball. Second, the club does not really hit the ball on this shot; it hits the sand under ball, which reduces control. Third, considerable force is needed to hit through the sand under the ball, but the distance the ball needs to travel is often very short, so it is easy to miscalculate how hard to swing the club. If swung too hard, the ball can fly entirely over the green, and even into another trap. If swung too easily, the ball might not get out of the sand trap at all, leading to another sand shot. Finally, with reduced control, the ball's bounce once it hits the green is less predictable, making it difficult to select the proper landing area on the way to the cup. Although hitting out of a sand trap is not impossible, the difficulties involved make it easy to see why you should be accurate with your approach shots to avoid sand traps in the first place.

There are some important things to know about golf rules that relate to making sand shots: (1) you must play the ball as it lies, even if it is deeply buried in the sand; (2) you are allowed to dig your feet into the sand as deeply as you like to improve footing, but you cannot build the sand up to improve your stance, and (3) your clubhead cannot touch the sand on your practice swings or backswing, so you can't cleverly move some sand out of the way as you bring the club back! Again, all this serves to increase the difficulty of playing out of a sand trap around the greens.

INSTRUCTOR DEMONSTRATION

Your course instructor will provide you with an explanation and demonstration of the key setup and performance cues for hitting greenside sand shots. Refer to Photos 8.1A through H. If you have questions, be sure to ask them before proceeding to the individualized task sequence.

SAND SHOTS FROM AROUND THE GREEN 97

Photo 8.1A
Sand shot setup and stance, view toward target

Photo 8.1B
Sand shot setup and stance, front view

MODULE 8

Photo 8.1C
Top of backswing

Photo 8.1D
Frontswing descent

SAND SHOTS FROM AROUND THE GREEN 99

Photo 8.1E
Contact point (note that the club hits the sand, not the ball)

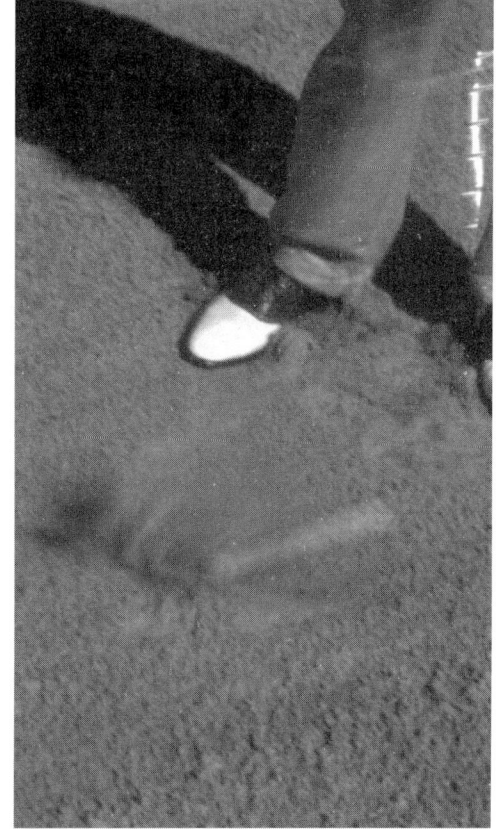

Photo 8.1F
Contact point, close-up

MODULE 8

Photo 8.1G
Frontswing, start of follow-through

Photo 8.1H
Follow-through

SETUP AND PERFORMANCE CUES

1. **Club choice:** Sand wedge or L-wedge
2. **Grip:** Interlocked or overlapped
3. **Stance:** Open, with some extra knee bend to keep you low
4. **Ball placement:** To the front if midline
5. **Hands alignment:** On midline, a bit lower than usual
6. **Clubface:** Strongly open to aiming line
7. **Aiming line:** Direct line to cup
8. **Contact spot:** Try to dig up a patch of sand that is 4 inches behind the ball and extends to 4 inches in front of the ball; DO NOT try to hit the ball directly with the clubface.
9. **Landing Spot:** Midpoint from front of trap to the cup; when in doubt, aim longer to reduce the risk of landing back in the trap
10. **Swing path:** Stay on aiming line all the way
11. **Swing Length:** Half- to three-quarters
12. **Follow-through:** Very important to finish with your *hands high*

COMPREHENSION TASK

Find a partner and demonstrate to each other the proper performance cues for the sand shot while standing on grass and *without hitting the ball*. Be sure to provide feedback to each other for correct and incorrect performance cues until both of you can correctly execute this stroke.

LEARNING TIPS

1. Sand shots are difficult because they call for strength and power on the swing, but generate relatively little distance, sometimes only 10 to 15 feet. You must learn to develop a feel for this shot, so do not be discouraged if it takes a long time to master it.

2. Remember, do not aim for the ball! Try to dig up a patch of sand that starts 4 inches behind the ball and extends to 4 inches in front of the ball. You should leave a sizeable divot in the sand trap where your ball was sitting.
3. The open stance and open clubface will feel awkward at first, but be confident that this is the correct setup for this shot.
4. Do not worry about hurting the sand trap. A correct sand shot will cause a lot of sand spray and leave a noticeable divot.
5. Be sure to rake the sand trap level where your ball was sitting, and also rake smooth any footprints you leave in the sand trap. This is a common courtesy among golfers.

READINESS DRILLS

8-1. Find a practice area that has long grass (about 3 to 4 inches long) with no one else around it. For these shots, **place** the ball so that it barely settles into the top of the grass. Pick an aiming line, but do not be concerned about a landing spot. Use your preshot routine and execute simulated sand shots that result in high loft and short distance. Your goal is to get the ball airborne on every shot, without concern for accuracy. Practice this until you can get the ball airborne consistently, and you have begun to develop a feel for this shot.

8-2. Hit 50 sand shots from a trap to a target cup on a green. Be sure to **place** each ball on the sand so that it does not create a small crater around the ball. Also, be sure to rake the sand trap level after each shot. Practice these shots until you can get the ball in the air and out of the trap consistently. Do not be concerned with accuracy at this point.

If you experience difficulty with the readiness drills, refer to the **Performance Cues** and review each cue as presented. If you still have difficulty, contact your course instructor to assist you in applying these techniques.

Common Errors and Their Correction

Error

Chunking the ball; taking up lots of sand, and the ball fails to get into flight.

Scullling the ball; hitting the ball first, not the sand, resulting in a very long distance.

Ball gets into flight, but it is much too short of landing spot (or rolls back into the trap).

Correction

1. Not swinging hard enough.
2. Insufficient follow-through, usually caused by not swinging hard enough.
3. Lifting your head, and then hitting too far in back of the ball.

1. Clubface not open enough.
2. No weight shift from back leg to front leg.

1. Not swinging hard enough.
2. Insufficient follow-through.
3. Wrists are not firm on contact with sand.

CRITERION TASK 8-1 (OPTIONAL)

Self-Checked

Find a practice green that has a sand trap around it and no one putting on it. For safety reasons, if more than one student is practicing this task, they should be hitting from the same trap to the same target. Because of the risk of sculling shots, do not practice from a spot that others are hitting toward, even if they are all the way across the green. Determine a flag stick or other target on the practice green to shoot for and place eight tees on the green around the target, 10 feet in all directions. This 20-foot circle will be your target.

Practice in blocks of 10 shots, making sure to place your ball on the sand each time; do not drop it down and make a crater around it. Each shot is worth up to 3 points. Score 1 point if the ball gets out of the sand trap on the fly. Score another point if the ball stops on the green outside the target circle. Score a third point if the ball stops on the green inside the target circle. Your block score is the sum total for each set of 10 shots. Try to get as many points as you can in each block until your scores are consistently at or above 15.

Personal Recording Form									
Block 1	Block 2	Block 3	Block 4	Block 5	Block 6	Block 7	Block 8	Block 9	Block 10
__/10	__/10	__/10	__/10	__/10	__/10	__/10	__/10	__/10	__/10

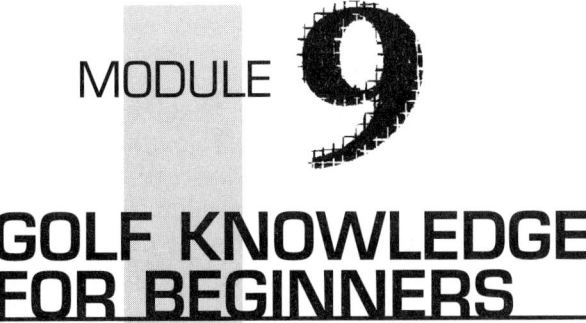

MODULE 9

GOLF KNOWLEDGE FOR BEGINNERS

Having completed the **Performance Skills Modules** of PSIS golf, we now turn to this **Golf Knowledge Module**, which will teach you the basic rules and etiquette of golf. This module can be completed in one or two class periods with a bit of out-of-class reading. If you have more days than that remaining until the end of the term, you might wish to go back and review the final skill performance task in each of the modules, perhaps making the criteria a bit more difficult than before. This will allow you to keep refining all those skills, thus increasing both your performance and enjoyment of the game.

INTRODUCTION

Modern golf is played by rules that have evolved for over 300 years, originating in Scotland. Many rules are written to provide a test of players' skills and creativity in the natural elements of earth and weather. The Scottish consider golf very much a game for all seasons and their sometimes seemingly stern rules are meant to alter the challenge to the player in accordance with naturally occurring changes in regional climatic conditions and weather.

With that stated, I encourage you to play the game of golf according to its traditional, official rules. You should also play for your enjoyment and that of others around you. To do this, you must have knowledge of the rules of golf and common golf course etiquette. The following section, *Golf Rules in Brief*, describes an appropriate form for beginning players. At this stage you do not need to know the full version of the rules or those that apply to strict competitive situations.

READING ASSIGNMENT

Once you have completed all the Performance Skill Modules, take time to carefully read the following *Golf Rules in Brief*, which includes Etiquette, and Playing Through. As you read, make marginal notes on the rules that are not clear to you. The next day in class ask your instructor to provide a longer explanation or, better yet, a *demonstration*. Many rules can be best understood by seeing and hearing how they are interpreted and applied.

When you have finished the reading and have no more questions for your instructor, complete the **Golf Knowledge Quiz** at the end of this module. *If the quiz will be used for grading, your instructor will inform you about how it will be evaluated.* If this quiz will not be used for grading, I recommend that you get a score of at least 80% and have your instructor review missed questions with you. In this way, you will have a good working knowledge of golf rules and etiquette before you complete PSIS golf and begin to play on your own.

GOLF RULES IN BRIEF

The following is a summary of some principal Rules of Golf. In case of doubt, refer to the complete rules published by the United States Golf Association and the Royal and Ancient Golf Club of St. Andrews.* The numbers in parentheses refer to sections in the complete rule book.

Etiquette

1. Don't move, talk, or stand close to or directly behind a player making a stroke.
2. Don't play until the group in front is out of the way.
3. Always play without delay. Leave the putting green as soon as all players in your group have holed out.
4. Invite faster groups to play through.
5. Replace divots. Smooth out footprints in bunkers.
6. Don't step on the line of another's putt.
7. Don't drop clubs on a putting green.
8. Replace the flag stick carefully in an upright position.
9. Leave the course in the condition in which you'd like to find it.

Match and Stroke Play

1. Put an identification mark on your ball. If you can't identify it as yours, it's lost. (27)

   If your ball becomes unfit for play, you may replace it, without penalty, on the hole where it becomes unfit or between holes. (5-3)

---

*Copyright © 2000 by the United States Golf Association and the Royal and Ancient Golf Club of St. Andrews.

2. Count your clubs. No more than 14. (4-4)

3. Don't use an artificial device or unusual equipment for gauging or measuring distance or conditions, or to give an artificial aid in gripping. (14-3)

4. Don't ask for advice from anyone except your partner or your caddie. Don't give advice to anyone except your partner. (8-1)

5. During a hole you may practice swing, but not play a practice stroke. Between holes you may practice chip and putt on or near the putting green of the hole last played or the tee of the next hole, but not from a hazard. (7-2)

6. Play without delay. (6-7)

Order of Play

1. On the first tee, the honor is determined by the order of the draw or, in the absence of a draw, by lot. (10)

2. In match play, the ball farther from the hole is played first. The winner of a hole tees off first on the next hole. If a player plays out of turn anywhere on the course, his opponent may require him to replay. (10-1)

3. In stroke play, the ball farthest from the hole is played first. The competitor with the lowest score on a hole tees off first on the next hole. There is generally no penalty for playing out of turn. (10-2)

4. In four-ball competitions, partners may play in the order they consider best. (30-3c and 31-5)

Teeing Ground

1. Tee off within two club lengths behind the front edges of the tee markers.

2. If you tee off outside this area, in match play there is no penalty, but your opponent may require you to replay the stroke. In stroke play, you incur a two-stroke penalty and must then play from within the proper area. (11-4)

Playing the Ball

1. Play the ball as it lies. (13-1)

    Don't touch the ball unless a rule permits. (18-2)

2. Play the course as you find it. Don't improve your lie, the area of your intended swing, or your line of play or a reasonable extension of that line beyond the hole by moving, bending, or breaking anything fixed or growing, except in fairly taking your stance or making your swing. Don't press anything down. (13-2)

    Don't build a stance. (13-3)

3. If your ball lies in a bunker or a water hazard, don't touch the ground in the bunker or the ground or water in the water hazard before the downswing. (13-4)

4. Strike at the ball with the clubhead. Don't push or scrape it. (14-1) If your club strikes the ball more than once in a single stroke, count the stroke and add a penalty stroke. (14-4)

5. If you play a wrong ball (except in a hazard), in match play you lose the hole. In stroke play you incur a two-stroke penalty and must then play the correct ball. (15)

Putting Green

1. Don't touch the line of your putt unless a rule permits. (16-1a)

    You may repair ball marks and old hole plugs on the line, but not spike marks. (16-1c)

2. You may lift, and if desired clean, your ball on the putting green. Always replace it on the exact spot. (16-1b)

3. Don't test the surface by scraping it or rolling a ball. (16-1d)

4. If your ball played from the putting green strikes the flag stick, in match play you lose the hole or in stroke play you incur a two-stroke penalty. (17-3)

5. Always hole out unless in match play your opponent concedes your putt. (2-4, 3-2, 16-2)

Ball at Rest Moved

1. If your ball is moved by you, your partner, or your caddie, except as permitted by the rules, or if it moves after you have addressed it, add a penalty stroke and replace your ball. (18-2)

2. If your ball is moved by someone else or another ball, replace it without penalty to you. (18)

Ball in Motion Deflected or Stopped

1. If your ball in motion is deflected or stopped by you, your partner, or your caddie, in match play you lose the hole. In stroke play you incur a two-stroke penalty and the ball is played as it lies. (19-2)

2. If your ball in motion is deflected or stopped by someone else, play your ball as it lies without penalty, except (a) in match play, if an opponent or his caddie deflects your ball, you may play it as it lies or replay it or (b) in stroke play, if your ball is deflected after a stroke on the putting green, you must replay. (19)

3. If your ball in motion is deflected or stopped by another ball at rest, play your ball as it lies. In stroke play, you incur a two-stroke penalty if your ball and the other ball were on the green before your stroke. Otherwise, there is no penalty. (19-5)

Lifting, Dropping, and Placing

1. If a ball to be lifted is to be replaced (e.g., when the ball is lifted on the putting green to clean it), its position must be marked. (20-1)

2. When dropping, stand erect, hold the ball at shoulder height and arm's length, and drop it. A ball to be dropped in a hazard must be dropped, and stay, in the hazard. (20-2a)

3. If a dropped ball strikes the player or his or her partner, caddie, or equipment, it must be re-dropped without penalty. (20-2a)

4. A dropped ball must be redropped if it rolls into a hazard, out of a hazard, onto a putting green, out of bounds or to a position where there is interference by the condition from which relief is taken (in case of immovable obstructions, abnormal ground conditions and wrong putting green) or comes to rest more than two club lengths from where it first struck a part of the course or nearer the hole than its original position, under Rules 24 and 25 or where the ball last crossed the water hazard margin under Rule 26-1. If the ball when re-dropped rolls into any position listed above, place it where it first struck a part of the course when redropped. (20-2c)

5. If the original lie of a ball to be replaced has been altered, place it in the nearest similar lie within one club length not nearer the hole, except in a bunker re-create the original lie and place it in that lie. (20-3b)

Ball Interfering with or Assisting Play

1. You may lift your ball if it might assist any other player. (22)

2. You may have any other ball lifted if it might interfere with your play or assist any other player. (22)

Loose Impediments

1. Loose impediments are natural objects (such as stones and leaves) not fixed or growing, not solidly embedded, and not adhering to the ball. (23)

2. You may move them unless the loose impediment and your ball lie in or touch the same hazard. (23-1)

3. If you move a loose impediment within one club length of your ball and your ball moves, the ball must be placed and (unless your ball was on the putting green) you incur a penalty stroke. (18-2c)

Obstructions

1. Obstructions are artificial (i.e., man-made) objects. Objects defining out-of-bounds such as fences posts or stakes and immovable artificial objects out of bounds are not obstructions. (24)

2. Movable obstructions (e.g., a rake) anywhere may be moved. If your ball moves, replace it without penalty. (24-1)

3. If an immovable obstruction interferes with your stance or swing, you may, except when your ball is in a water hazard, drop within *one* club length of the nearest point of relief not nearer the hole. In a bunker drop in the bunker, and on the putting green, place in the nearest position that affords relief, not nearer the hole; there is no relief for intervention on your line of play unless your ball and the obstruction are on the green. (24-2)

4. If your ball is lost in an immovable obstruction (except where the entrance is in a water hazard) take the same relief based on the point where the balled entered the obstruction. (24-2c)

Abnormal Ground Conditions

1. If your ball is in an abnormal ground condition (casual water, ground under repair or, a hole, cast or runway made by a burrowing animal, you may drop without penalty within one club length of the nearest point of relief not nearer the hole, except (a) in a bunker drop in the nearest position in the bunker, or under penalty of one stroke, drop any distance behind the hazard or (b) on the putting green place at the nearest point of relief. (25-1b)

2. If your ball is lost in an abnormal ground condition (except in a water hazard), take the same relief based on the point where the ball last crossed the margin of the area. (25-1c)

Water Hazards

1. If your ball is in a water hazard, you may play the ball as it lies or, under penalty of one stroke,

    - replay the shot, or

    - drop any distance behind the water hazard keeping the point at which the original ball last crossed the margin of the water hazard directly between the hole and the spot on which the ball is dropped. (26-1ab)

2. If your ball is in a lateral water hazard, you may proceed as above or, under penalty of one stroke, you may also drop within two club-lengths or, and not nearer the hole than,

    - the point where the ball last crossed the margin of the hazard or

    - a point on the opposite side of the hazard equal distance from the hole. (26-1c)

Lost or Out of Bounds

1. If your ball may be lost outside a water hazard or out of bounds, you may play a provisional ball before you go forward to look for the original, provided you announce your intention to do so. If your original ball turns out to be in a water hazard or is found outside a water hazard, you must abandon the provisional ball. (27-2)

2. If your ball is lost outside a water hazard or is out of bounds, add one penalty stroke and play the provisional or, if you did not play a provisional, replay the shot. (27-1)

Unplayable

1. If you believe your ball is unplayable outside a water hazard, you may, under penalty of one stroke,

- replay the shot

- drop within two club-lengths of where the ball lies not nearer the hole, or

- drop any distance behind the point where the ball lay (keeping that point directly between the hole and the spot on which the ball is dropped).

If your ball is in a bunker you may proceed as above, except that, if you are dropping within two club-lengths or back on a line, you must drop to the bunker.

The preceding *Golf Rules in Brief* is reprinted with permission of the United States Golf Association. To order the complete *Rules of Golf*, contact the USGA Order Department at 1-800-336-4446.

WINTER RULES (UNOFFICIAL)

Winter Rules may apply under two conditions: (1) at those times of the year when the turf on the golf course has bare spots or is unusually hard and (2) when temporary conditions make normal play extremely difficult (usually weather related). If it is an informal competition, players may declare by mutual agreement that Winter Rules are in effect. If it is a formal competition, only the Competition Director or Committee can make such a declaration. The following are some of the most typical Winter Rules.

1. Any ball that lands outside the fairway (in the rough) is played *as it lies* and is subject to all regular rules of play.

2. Any ball that lies in the fairway may be *rolled with the clubhead* no more than 1 foot from where it lies to provide a better hitting surface.

3. Unless rule 5 applies, no ball may be lifted and dropped or placed back on the ground for hitting.

4. Players may not roll the ball onto a tuft of grass or mound that, in effect, provides a hitting tee for the next shot.

5. At any time, a ball with mud or other impediments on it may be lifted, cleaned, and dropped back for play. The drop must follow the procedures stated in the rules, unless dropping it will result in the impediment occurring again. It that case, it is permissible to place the ball back on the ground for play.

PLAYING THROUGH

Not all players or groups take the same amount of time to complete a round of golf. Frequently, a faster player or group will catch up to a slower player or group on the course. For these descriptions, a slow player or group is defined a one that is more than **two completed shots** behind the player or group in front of them.

If you are more than two shots behind the group in front of you, and the group behind you is regularly waiting to play, you should allow them to *play through* with the following procedure.

1. Allow everyone in your group to complete his or her current shot.
2. Signal (usually a wave) the group behind you to play through.
3. Move away from the anticipated landing area for that group's next shots.
4. Allow each player to complete his or her shot to catch up.
5. Then allow each person to take the needed shots to get ahead of you *and* to get *out of range* of your next shot.
6. If you are on the green and signal a group to play through, you may wish to complete the hole after they have made their approach shots and are walking to the green. You can then allow them to tee off ahead of you on the next hole.

GOLF KNOWLEDGE QUIZ

Your name _____ Today's date _____

Directions: Be sure that you have read the *Golf Rules in Brief* and additional sections completely and have asked your instructor to clarify those points that you did not understand. Give the completed quiz to your instructor, who will check your answers. **The mastery criterion for this quiz is _____ correct answers. You may repeat the quiz until you have reached the criterion.**

Circle (T)rue or (F)alse for each statement below.

1. T F Your club may not touch the ground before making contact when your ball rests in a bunker or hazard.

2. T F You may pick up, mark, and clean your ball when it rests on the putting green.

3. T F You may remove loose impediments to hitting your ball if your ball is not in a hazard.

4. T F The ball farthest from the hole is always played first.

5. T F Your ball is lost, and you have played a provisional ball. You do not have to take a penalty stroke.

6. T F Having the honor means going first from the tee.

7. T F You can tee off from any place behind the tee markers.

8. T F When playing Winter Rules, you may improve your lie at any time.

9. T F It is permissible for your ball to hit the flag stick if the shot was taken from off the green.

10. T F It is good etiquette to play through slower groups as soon as you are able.

11. T F The legal limit on the number of clubs in your bag is 14.

12. T F You are permitted to drop your ball within one club length in any direction from an immovable obstruction.

13. T F If your ball is in "ground under repair," you may drop it without incurring a penalty.

14. T F It is OK to stand behind another player while he or she makes a stroke.

15. T F When playing Winter Rules, you may clean your ball any time it has an impediment on it.

16. T F You are dropping your ball from a sand bunker, and it rolls out of the bunker after it is dropped. This is your "good luck," and you may play the ball from its new position.

17. T F Out-of-bounds markers are movable, therefore, it is permissible to move one in order to make your shot.

18. T F In Winter Rules, a ball in the rough is subject to all regular rules.

19. T F Your ball is on the green, but your partner's ball is closer to the hole (not on the green). Your partner plays first.

20. T F The ball must be struck with the clubhead.

Personal Progress Chart for PSIS Golf

Module															
9	Golf Knowledge Quiz														
8	Sand Shots (Optional)														
7	Tee Shots														
6	Approach Shots														
5	Around the Green														
4	Complete Golf Swing														
3	Putting														
2	Golf Basics														
1	Stretching														
	Weeks in Class	1	2	3	4	5	6	7	8	9	10	11	12	13	14	15